# Tipbook

# Cello

*The Complete Guide*

Hugo Pinksterboer

# Tipbook
# Cello

*The Complete Guide*

HAL•LEONARD®

## The Complete Guide to Your Instrument!

First edition published in 2002 by
The Tipbook Company bv, The Netherlands
Third edition published in 2008 by
Hal Leonard Books
An Imprint of Hal Leonard Corporation
7777 West Bluemound Road
Milwaukee, WI 53213

Trade Book Division Editorial Offices
19 West 21st Street, New York, NY 10010


Printed in the United States of America


Book design by Gijs Bierenbroodspot


Library of Congress Cataloging-in-Publication Data

Pinksterboer, Hugo.
  Tipbook cello : the complete guide / Hugo Pinksterboer. -- 4th ed.
      p. cm.
  "Complete guide to your instrument."
  Includes index.
  ISBN 978-1-4234-5623-0 (pbk.)
  1. Violoncello.  I. Title.
  ML910.P46 2008
  787.4--dc22
                                    2008040097


www.halleonard.com

## Thanks!

For their information, their expertise, their time, and their help we'd like to thank the following musicians, teachers, technicians, and other bowed instrument experts:

Edward C. Campbell (violin maker, PA), Duane Lightner (Discount String Center, IN), Lang Shen (Knilling String Instruments, MO), David Rivinus (violin maker, OR), Caryn Patterson (Super-Sensitive Strings, FL), Heinz Kovacs (Thomastik-Infeld, Austria), Sandy Neill (D'Addario, NY), Volker Müller-Zierach (Pirastro, Germany), Klaus Clement (Höfner, Germany), David Nereson, Barbara Van Itallie (Violin Society of America), Kim Rodney and Frederik Habel (Gewa, Germany), Barbara Woldring, Michaël van Berkum (violin maker), Ben de Ligt, Levent Aslan, Isabelle van Keulen, Nello Mirando, Theo Olof, Mies Albarda (European String Teachers Association (ESTA/ARCO), Jaap Bolink (violin maker), Gijs van Ulsen, Taner Erkek, Harm van der Geest, Siard de Jong, Fred Lindeman (violin maker), Annelies Steinhauer (violin maker), Eduard van Tongeren (violin maker), Helena and Jelle van Tongeren, Tom van Berkel, Bas van den Broek, and Fred Pinksterboer.

We also wish to thank Frank Pameijer for his musical help in making the Tipcode-movies.

The cello on the cover is played by Davina Cowan.

V

## About the Author

Journalist, writer and musician **Hugo Pinksterboer**, author of The Tipbook Series, wrote hundreds of interviews and instrument reviews as well as numerous DVD, CD, and book reviews for a wide variety of music magazines.

## About the Designer

Illustrator, designer, and musician **Gijs Bierenbroodspot** has worked as an art director for a wide variety of magazines and has developed numerous ad campaigns. While searching in vain for information about saxophone mouthpieces, he got the idea for this series of books on music and musical instruments. He is responsible for the layout and the illustrations for all of the Tipbooks.

## Acknowledgments

Cover photo: René Vervloet
Editors: Robert L. Doerschuk, Michael J. Collins, and Meg Clark
Proofreader: Nancy Bishop

## Anything missing?

Any omissions? Any areas that could be improved? Please go to www.tipbook.com to contact us, or send an email to info@tipbook.com. Thanks!

# Contents

# *Introduction*

*Have you just started playing? Are you thinking about buying a cello? Or do you want to learn more about the instrument you already have? If so, this book will tell you everything you need to know. About buying or renting an instrument, about tailpieces, tuning pegs, bridges, and fingerboards, about bows, strings, and tuning. About the best way to maintain your instrument, about the history of the cello, about its family, and much, much more.*

Having read this Tipbook, you'll be able to get the most out of your instrument, to buy the best cello you can, and to easily grasp any other literature on the subject, from books and magazines to Internet publications.

### The first four chapters
If you have just started playing, or haven't yet begun, pay particular attention to the first four chapters. They explain the basics of the instrument and the bow, and inform you on learning to play the cello, cello practicing, and buying or renting an instrument. This information also fully prepares you to read the rest of the book.

### Advanced players
Advanced players can skip ahead to Chapter 5, where you find everything you need to know to make an informed choice when you're going to buy or rent a cello. Chapters 6 and 7 offer similar

information on selecting strings, bows, and rosins. Chapter 8 deals with accessories such as cases and bags, cello stands, and wolf tone suppressors.

### Tuning and maintenance

Chapters 9 and 10 help you get the best out of your instrument by offering helpful information on tuning and maintaining your precious cello.

### Background information

The final chapters offer essential reading material on the history of the cello, the family of the instrument, the way it is made, and on its makers.

### US dollars

Please note that all price indications listed on the following pages are based on estimated street prices in US dollars.

### Glossary

The glossary at the end of the book briefly explains most of the terms you'll come across as a cellist. Also included are an index of terms, and a couple of pages for essential notes on your equipment.

### Practicing

As an extra, this edition of *Tipbook Cello* provides you with a general chapter on effective practicing. Enjoy!


— **Hugo Pinksterboer**

# See and Hear What You Read with Tipcodes

*www.tipbook.com*

**In addition to the many illustrations on the following pages, Tipbooks offer you a new way to see —and even hear — what you are reading about. The Tipcodes that you will come across throughout this book give you access to short movies, soundtracks, and other additional information at www.tipbook.com.**

How it works is very simple. The main paragraph on page 123 deals with fitting new strings on your instrument. On that same page, you'll find *Tipcode CELLO-019*.

**TIPCODE**

**Tipcode CELLO-019**
*Fitting a string (again, shown on a violin).*

Type in that code on the Tipcode page at www.tipbook.com and you will see a short movie that shows you how to do this.

### Enter code, watch movie

You enter the Tipcode below the movie window on the Tipcode page. In most cases, you will then see the relevant images within five to ten seconds. Tipcodes activate a short movie, sound, or both, or a series of photos.

### Tipcode list

For your convenience, the Tipcodes presented in this book are also listed on page 192.

### Quick start

The Tipcode movies, photo series, and soundtracks are designed so that they start quickly. If you miss something the first time, you

First, make your selection: Tipcode, chords and fingering charts, or the glossary.

The Tipcode window displays videos, fingering charts, chords, or a glossary of the terms used in this book.

Enter a Tipcode here and click on the button. Want to see it again? Click again.

These links take you directly to other interesting sites.

can of course repeat them. And if it all happens too fast, use the pause button below the movie window.

### Plug-ins
If the software you need to view the videos is not yet installed on your computer, you'll automatically be told which software you need, and where you can download it. This software is free. Questions? Check out 'About this site' at www.tipbook.com.

### Still more at www.tipbook.com
You can find even more information at www.tipbook.com. For instance, you can look up words in the glossaries of *all* the Tipbooks published to date. There are chord diagrams for guitarists and pianists; fingering charts for saxophonists, clarinetists, and flutists; and rudiments for drummers. Also included are links to most of the websites mentioned in the *Want to Know More?* section of each Tipbook.

# 1

# A Cellist?

*As a cellist, you can play solo, all by yourself, or in a duet with a pianist or another cellist. You can also play in a symphony orchestra, with dozens of other musicians. There are countless other types of groups and ensembles you can join as well, playing classical music, or perhaps jazz, or yet another style of music. A chapter about all the things you can do as a cellist.*

At first sight, cellos look a lot like violins. They're a lot bigger, though, and they sound lower. When you play the cello, it rests between your legs, standing on a rod.

### String instrument
The cello is a *string instrument*, just like the violin. You play these instruments by drawing a bow across the strings. That's why they're also known as *bowed instruments*.

### The voice
The sound of a cello is often said to resemble the human voice. The highest sounding string of the cello is even known as the *chanterelle* — in English, the singing string.

### Wide range
That is just one of the reasons why cellists can be found in so many different groups and ensembles. Another is that their instrument can sound both very low and extremely high: The cello has a very wide *range*. Also, its tone blends well with a wide variety of instruments, from woodwinds such as the flute or the clarinet, to the piano, the accordion, other string instruments, and — of course — the human voice.

**TIPCODE**

*Tipcode CELLO-001*
*This Tipcode demonstrates the*
*wide range of the instrument.*

### Different styles
Most cellists play classical music, but you'll find them in many other styles too — in folk music from different countries, in gypsy music, the tango and French chansons, in jazz and pop, and in avant-garde music, for example.

**Tipcode CELLO-002**
The cello can be played in a wide
variety of styles of music. Here's a
bit of classical playing and some
gypsy-style music.

AUDIO

TIPCODE

### Classical music

There is a wide variety of classical cello music available. That's not surprising, because the instrument has been around for centuries. All in all there is so much cello music that you couldn't play it in a lifetime.

This is how
you play the
cello.

3

### Large and small

Classical music can be played in large and small orchestras, in quartets, and in many other kinds of groups and ensembles. Here are some examples.

### Symphony orchestra

The strings are the main voices of the largest orchestra of all, the symphony orchestra, which has a total of fifty to a hundred or more members. In a symphony orchestra, the cellists are usually seated to the right of the conductor. On the conductor's immediate right is the *principal cellist*, who leads the cello section. On the conductor's left hand is the *concertmaster*, a violinist who is the leader of the entire orchestra.

### String sections

The cellists are one of the five groups of string instrument players in the orchestra. The largest group is the violinists, of whom there may be thirty or more, divided into *first* and *second violinists*. The *violists*, a smaller string section, play the slightly bigger and lower-sounding *viola*. Behind the cellists are the bassists. Their instrument, the *double bass*, is one of the lowest voices of the orchestra.

*An example of the arrangement of the instruments in a symphony orchestra. The cellos are nearly always at the front, to the right of the conductor.*

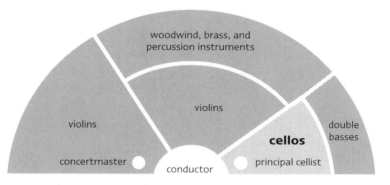

### String sections and orchestras

The four string sections of a symphony orchestra are not unlike the different groups of singers in a choir: sopranos, altos, tenors (the cellists), and basses. So it shouldn't be a surprise that there are string orchestras too, made up of string players only.

4

### Cello orchestras

Also, there's music written or adapted for cello orchestras, with fifty or even more cellists, and for smaller cello ensembles, with songs and compositions that range from tangos to Spanish folk songs, Christmas carols, hymns, and even heavy-metal hits.

### Other musicians

In a symphony orchestra you'll find other musicians as well, such as brasswind players (playing trumpet, French horn, trombone, and other instruments), woodwind players (clarinet, flute, oboe, bassoon, and so on), percussionists (snare drums, tympani, cymbals), harpists, a pianist… As you can see, the louder instruments, such as the trumpets and percussion instruments, are further toward the back; the strings are closer to the audience.

### String quartet

A lot of classical music has been written for smaller groups too. A well-known and very popular ensemble is the string quartet, for instance, with two violinists, a violist, and a cellist.
A string quintet has two cellists or two violists. Piano trios are written for piano, violin, and cello; for a piano quartet you add a viola.

*A few bars from a string quartet (W. A. Mozart); music for two violins, viola, and cello.*

5

### Duo and solo

There is also a lot of cello music for duos. The most popular combination is cello and piano, but you can also play with another cellist, for example, or with a clarinetist or an accordion player. And there are pieces that are meant to be played solo — just a cello, and nothing else. Of course, that's a different type of solo playing than when you play 'solo' cello accompanied by a full orchestra.

**TIP**

### Cello or violoncello?

Most musicians call a cello a cello, but some use the older name of the instrument, violoncello. In the past, the cello has had many other names as well. You'll find more about this and the instrument's history in Chapter 11, Back in Time.

### Sello or chello?

The cello is an Italian instrument, originally. That's why most musicians pronounce its name as 'chello,' as Italians would say it. Others say 'sello,' and both are right. Similarly, if you're talking about more than one cello, you can say 'celli' — the Italian way — or 'cellos.'

# 2

# A Quick Tour

A cello has a body, a neck, and a fingerboard, four strings,
four pegs, and a whole list of other parts. A chapter about
what everything's called, what it's for and where to find it,
and about cellos for children.

The main part of the cello, the *body*, is the soundbox of the instrument: It amplifies the sound of the strings. Without the body, you would hardly hear yourself play.

### Top and back
The *top* and the *back* of the body are noticeably arched. The top is the most important part for the sound of the instrument. It has two large *f*-shaped *soundholes*, also known as *f-holes*.

### Tuning pegs
You tune the strings using the *pegs* or *tuning pegs*. There is one for each string, at the top of the instrument, fitted in the *pegbox*.

### Scroll and volute
The head of the instrument is known as the *scroll*, with the typically spiral-shaped *volute* on top of it.

### Fingerboard
The strings run along the *fingerboard* onto which you press your fingers to *stop the strings*. If you stop a string you make it shorter, so to speak. This makes the string produce a higher note.

TIPCODE

**Tipcode CELLO-003**
This Tipcode demonstrates how stopping a string makes it produce a higher note.

### The neck
The fingerboard is a thin, dark plank that's glued to the neck. The neck runs from the scroll to the body. The fingerboard is quite a bit longer: A large part juts out over the body.

8

volute

scroll

pegbox

tuning pegs

nut

cheek

neck

fingerboard

strings

heel

back button

upper bout

purfling

top

channel

rib

waist
(C-bout)

bridge

*f*-hole

fine tuner

lower bout

saddle

tailpiece

end pin, spike,
or rod

*A cello.*

### Nut

At the top of the fingerboard, the strings run over a small ridge called the *nut*.

### The bridge

About halfway down the body, the strings run over the *bridge*, a thin piece of wood that's much lighter in color than the rest of the cello. When you play, you make the strings vibrate with your *bow*. The bridge passes on those vibrations to the top. The top, together with the rest of the body, amplifies the sound.

### Feet

The bridge stands on the top on its two *feet*, without the help of glue or screws. The pressure of the strings keeps it from falling over.

### Tailpiece and fine tuners

The strings are attached to the pegs at one end and to the *tailpiece* at the other. Inside the tailpiece there are often one or more *fine tuners*, which allow you to tune your cello more easily and precisely than with the big wooden tuning pegs.

*The end pin: a button or plug, screw, and a rod.*

saddle

tailpiece loop

button or plug

rod

screw

### Button, loop, and saddle

The tailpiece is attached to the *button* or *end button* with the *tailpiece loop*. To make sure this loop doesn't damage the body, it runs over the *saddle* or *bottom nut*.

### Fittings

The tailpiece, pegs, and end pin plug are collectively known as the *fittings* or the *trim*.

### End pin

The *end pin* takes most of the weight of the cello, when you play. Adjusting its height is simply a matter of how far you pull the rod out. When you're done playing, you push the rod back into the instrument.

### Purfling

The inlaid *purfling* runs along the edge of the body. It is usually made of three narrow strips of wood — two ebony or dark dyed strips, and a lighter wood in between.

### Channel

From the edge, the top usually dips a little, before the upward arching begins. This 'valley' is called the *channel*. The back has almost the same shape.

### Heel and neck base

The semicircular part that sticks out at the top of the back is called the *heel* or the *button*. The *neck base* is the part of the neck that links it to the body

neck base

heel

11

# INSIDE

There is plenty to see inside a cello too, from the sound post to the bass bar, the maker's label, and a number of small wooden blocks.

### The sound post

If you look through the *f*-hole at the treble side of the instrument (by the thinnest string), you can see a length of round wood, wedged between the top and the back. That's the *sound post*. Without its sound post, a cello would sound very thin or hollow.

### The bass bar

Near the other *f*-hole, on the bass side, is the *bass bar*. This strengthens the top and it enhances the lower frequencies of the instrument. If you can take the rod of the end pin out of your instrument, you'll be able to see both the bass bar and the sound post through the hole in the end pin plug.

*The bass bar and sound post are important to the sound of a cello.*

bass bar

sound post

12

**TIP**

### The label

If you look down the f-hole on the bass side, you may see the violin maker's label. Violin maker? Yes: The people who make cellos are known as violin makers. Usually, they make violins, violas, and cellos, and sometimes double basses too. Violin makers are also referred to as luthiers.

## THE BOW

To play the cello you need a bow. The quality of the bow is as important as the quality of the instrument itself.

### Bow hair and stick

The *bow hair* — usually more than two hundred hairs — almost always comes from a horse's tail. One end of the hair is held in place inside the *head* or *tip*, at the top end of the *stick* or *bow stick*. The other end is held in place inside the *frog*.

### Tension the hair

Before you play, you have to tension the hair by turning the *screw button* clockwise. After you have finished playing, turn the screw button counterclockwise until the hair goes slack. If you don't, the stick's elasticity will gradually decrease.

### Bow grip

You hold the bow at the (*bow*) *grip*, often made of leather, and

**13**

the *winding*, usually made of very thin metal wire. Apart from improving your bow hold, this also protects the wood.

### Rosin

For the bow to do its job properly, you need to rub the hair with a piece of *rosin*. Rosin makes the bow hair slightly sticky. Without it, sliding the bow across the strings will hardly produce a sound.

## STRINGS AND CLEFS

A cello has four strings. Most cellists use strings with a steel core; others prefer strings with a synthetic or a gut core. If you take a closer look, you can see that the strings are usually wound with ultra-thin metal ribbon.

### The notes

The cello strings are tuned to the notes C, G, D, and A, as shown on the piano keyboard below. The C is the lowest sounding string; the thin A-string is the highest.

*The four cello strings and the range of the instrument, pictured on a piano keyboard.*

### Very low, very high

If you go from the lowest to the very highest note you can play on a cello, you will span more than five octaves. (An octave is eight white keys on a piano.) This means that a cello has a wider range than most other instruments.

14

## A3

As you can see in the illustration, the A-string of a cello sounds the same pitch as the A to the left of the Middle C. This particular A is indicated as A3. It sounds one octave lower than A4, the pitch to which most musicians tune their instruments.

### Lower case

In classical literature, you may find A3 being indicated with the lower-case letter a, and A4 as a'.

**TIP**

## Clefs

If you take another look at the music on page 5, you'll see that each stave is marked with a different symbol for each different instrument. This symbol is called a *clef.*
The music for the violins is written using the *treble clef* or *G clef.* The music for the cello has a *bass clef* or *F clef,* and the *viola* (or *alto violin*) uses the *alto clef.* With each clef, the lines of the staff indicate different notes.

## All three

Because of the wide range of the instrument, you can't write cello music using the bass clef alone. The highest notes on the cello are written using the treble clef — just like the violin — and for in-between notes there's the *tenor clef* (a *C clef* with Middle C on the second line from the top).
As a cellist, you will eventually have to learn to read music in these three clefs.

# CHILDREN'S INSTRUMENTS

A full-size cello is too big for most children under twelve to fourteen years of age. That's why there are cellos in small or *fractional sizes.*

15

### Full-size cello

An 'adult' cello is usually referred to as a *full-size cello*. On paper this is often indicated as a ¾ cello. The illustrations on these pages show that a ½ cello is not really half as big as a ¼ instrument. Besides the ones shown here, there are other fractional sizes as well.

### No rules

There are no absolute rules for which size goes with which age. One six-year-old might be better off with ¼ cello while another child of that age needs a ½ instrument. That's why you always need to 'fit' a cello, and the same goes for the bow. A teacher will know how, and so will a good violin dealer or maker. Not only the child's finger and arm lengths count, but also factors such as the strength of his or her fingers.

*The most popular cello sizes and their average string lengths (measured from nut to bridge).*

| ¹/₈ | ¹/₈ | ¹/₂ |
|---|---|---|
| (19.29"/490mm) | (21.06"/535mm) | (23.62"/600mm) |

16

### Variations

The exact sizes of the instruments also vary: For example, one ½ cello may be slightly bigger than the other.

### Smaller

As smaller cellos have a 'smaller' tone, you shouldn't play an instrument that is 'too small' for you. Having said that, if you're absolutely in love with the sound of your ⅞ cello, you may prefer that instrument to a full-size — until you find one you like even better...

**3/4**
(25.00"/635mm)

**7/8**
(26.34"/670mm)

**4/4**
(27.36"/695mm)

# 3

# Learning to Play

The cello may not be the easiest instrument to get started on, but it won't take years before you can perform on it. A chapter about learning to play, lessons, and practicing.

Anyone can play any note on a piano: Just hit the right key, and it sounds. On a cello it's a bit harder. Producing a nice and even tone by drawing the bow over the strings will definitely take you some time.

### Pizzicato

You can also play the cello by plucking the strings with your fingers. This is known as *pizzicato.* Teachers may start their students off with this technique to get them accustomed to using the left hand first.

**TIPCODE**

**Tipcode CELLO-004**
Play this Tipcode to see a cellist plucking the strings: pizzicato!

### The right place

To play the cello in tune, you have to put your left-hand fingers in exactly the right places on the fingerboard. This too takes time to learn.

### Stickers

Of course, teachers have developed various techniques to make learning the cello less difficult than it may sound here — and there are thousands of young cellists to demonstrate that it can be done. One of the techniques used is simply to mark the positions where to put your left hand on the fingerboard with stickers.

# LESSONS

20

If you take cello lessons, you'll learn about everything connected

*Finding the exact place...*

with playing the instrument — from bowing technique and reading music to good posture.

### Finding a teacher

Are your looking for a private teacher? Violin makers and dealers may be able to refer you to a cello teacher, and music stores may have teachers on staff. You can also consult your local Musicians' Union or the orchestra teacher at a high school in your vicinity, check the classified ads in newspapers and in music magazines, or consult the *Yellow Pages*. Teachers can also be found on the Internet (see page 196 for some starting points). Some players have found great teachers in musicians they have seen in performance.

**21**

### Prices
Professional private teachers will usually charge between twenty-five and seventy-five dollars per hour. Some make house calls, for which you'll pay extra.

### Group or individual lessons
Instead of taking individual lessons, you can also go for group lessons if that's an option in your vicinity. Private lessons are more expensive, but can be tailored exactly to your needs.

### Collectives
You also may want to check whether there are any teachers' collectives or music schools in your area. These collectives may offer extras such as ensemble playing, master classes, and clinics in a wide variety of styles and at various levels.

### Questions, questions
On your first visit to a teacher, don't simply ask how much it costs. Here are some other useful questions.

- Is an **introductory lesson** included? This is a good way to find out how well you get on with the teacher and, for that matter, with the instrument.

- Is the teacher interested in taking you on as a student if you are just doing it for the fun of it, or are you expected to practice **at least three hours** a day?

- Do you have to make a large investment in method books right away, or is **course material provided**?

- Can you **record your lessons**, so that you can listen at home to how you sound, and once more to what has been said?

TIP

### More information
*For more information on assessing a teacher and all related subjects, please consult* Tipbook Music For Kids and Teens, A Guide For Parents *(see page 207).*

22

- Is this teacher going to make you practice scales for two years, or will you be **pushed onto a stage** as soon as possible?

- For more information, see *Tipbook Music For Kids* (page 207).

## PRACTICE

How long should you practice? That depends on your talent and on what you want to achieve. As an indication: Half an hour a day usually results in steady progress. If playing half an hour at a stretch seems too long, try dividing it up into two quarter-hour sessions, or three of ten minutes each.

### Silent practicing
Cellos don't make a lot of noise, but they are loud enough to bother other people when you are practicing. There are various ways to overcome this.

### Practice mute
First of all, you can buy a *practice mute*, available in wood, metal, or rubber, for some ten to fifteen dollars. You simply slide this short, fat 'comb' onto the bridge of your cello, where it effectively mutes most of the sound you produce — so it's best not to use one if you're working on your tone. Other types of mutes are covered in Chapter 8.

**Tipcode CELLO-005**
*A practice mute, demonstrated on a violin, effectively reduces the instrument's volume.*

TIPCODE

23

A practice mute.

### Electric cello

If you want to produce even less sound, you may want to invest in an electric cello. Some of these instruments have been specifically designed for silent practicing. You play them using a pair of headphones; the extremely modest sound of the strings is amplified by a small built-in amp. A special input allows you to hook up a CD player, for instance, so you can play along with prerecorded music. There's more on electric cellos in Chapter 12, *The Family*.

### On CD

Most cello music is played together with other string instruments, with a piano, or with a complete orchestra. There's an easy way to get hold of those other musicians, without having to invite them all: For instance, you can get special practice CDs with the same

TIP

### Your computer

There are also CD-ROMs you can play along to. Of course, you will need to have a computer handy. Some CD-ROMs even let you decide how fast a piece should be played or whether you want to mute the cello part.

24

piece of music recorded three times. The first time very slowly with piano and cello, so that you can play along with the cellist. The next time faster with just the piano. Then once more with a full orchestra, in the tempo in which the piece is supposed to be played. These CDs usually come with sheet music.

**25**

### Metronome

Most pieces of music are supposed to be played in the same tempo from beginning to end. Playing with a metronome now and then helps you to learn how to play at a constant tempo. A metronome is a small mechanical or electronic device that ticks or bleeps out a steady adjustable pulse, so you can tell immediately if you're dragging or speeding.

*Two mechanical metronomes and two electronic ones.*

### Recording your lessons

If you record your lessons, you can listen to what was said, and especially how you sounded, when you get home. Hearing yourself play is very helpful. That's why many musicians record themselves. All you need is a portable recording device with a built-in microphone — although better equipment yields better and more enjoyable results.

### More information

If you want to learn more about making your practice sessions effective and fun, please check out Tips On Practicing on pages 161–163.

**26**

### Listen and play

Finally, visit festivals, concerts, and other performances. Go watch and listen to orchestras, string quartets, and other groups. One of the best ways to learn to play is seeing other musicians at work. Living legends or local amateurs — every concert's a learning experience. And the best way to learn to play? Play a lot!

# 4

# Buying or Renting?

What does a cello cost? Somewhere between a few
hundred and a few million dollars... A guide to cello
prices, and to buying or renting an instrument.

Children under twelve often start off on a rented cello, which can be easily exchanged for a larger size after you've grown a bit. Even if you are well beyond that age, renting a cello can be a good way to start, to find out either if you like playing the instrument at all, or if you like a specific instrument. For example, you may rent a forty-thousand-dollar cello for some six hundred dollars per month.

## Rental fees

You can rent a full-sized student cello from around forty dollars a month, complete with bow and case, and some companies even rent out instruments for some hundred and fifty dollars for an academic year. Not all companies have lower rental fees for fractional instruments.

## The basics

It is impossible to provide a detailed description of the infinite amount of different plans, terms, and conditions you will likely encounter when you decide to rent an instrument. But here are the basics:

• Many rental plans are actually **rent-to-own plans**: The instrument is yours once the periodic payments you've made equal the list price. Note that this list price will usually be higher than what you would have paid had you just bought the instrument outright — which explains why most of these plans are interest free.
The profit is in the difference between the standard, discounted street, or 'going' price, and the list price.

• Most of these rent-to-own or **hire-purchase plans** also have an option to buy the instrument before you're fully paid up; if you choose to buy the instrument, your rent paid to date will usually be applied to the instrument.

• With a **lease plan** — also known as a straight rental plan or **rent-to-rent plan** — you simply keep paying rent until you return the instrument. Rates are usually lower on these plans than those of rent-to-own plans. With these plans, renting for a long period of time will, of course, be more expensive than buying the instrument.

### Maintenance and insurance

Maintenance is usually included in the rental fee, but some plans offer it as a separate expense. The main thing is to make sure you don't have to worry about it. Insurance may be included as well. Make sure you understand what is and isn't covered under your lease or rental plan. Insurance rates for student instruments are usually under ten dollars per month.

- Does the fee **include** instrument set-up, maintenance, and finance or bank charges?

- If **insurance** is included, does it also cover theft and loss?

- Do you get a **replacement instrument** if yours needs maintenance?

- Do you have to pay an **origination fee**, an application fee, or a deposit? These costs are usually non-refundable; they often may be applied to the rental, however.

- Is there a **reconditioning fee**, a stocking fee, or a depreciation fee when you return the instrument?

- Always ask if you get a **new or a used** (rental-return) instrument.

- Note that stores may ask for a **deposit** or require your **credit card details**.

---

### Try before you buy

*It's also possible to rent a more expensive instrument, so you can take your time to assess its quality. For example, you may rent a forty-thousand-dollar cello for six hundred dollars per month (i.e., 1.5% of the list price).*

**TIP**

---

## BUYING A CELLO?

If you're looking for a decent, good-sounding cello that you can enjoy playing for a number of years, many dealers and teachers

31

will tell you to spend some fourteen hundred to two thousand dollars or more, and add at least another three to four hundred for a basic bow and a case.

### Cheaper instruments

Of course, plenty of people have had years of fun playing a much cheaper instrument. After all, you can buy a complete *outfit* (cello, bow, and case) for as little as four hundred dollars, or even less. That said, there are cheap cellos that are barely playable unless you have a lot of work done to them—even if they are labeled 'shop adjusted.'

### Shop adjustment

Basically, every production cello needs an additional shop adjustment before it can be played. This adjustment, commonly known as *setting up the instrument*, includes making sure that the bridge, nut, sound post, fingerboard, and tuning pegs perfectly fit the instrument.

### Better, finer, richer

If you buy a more expensive cello, the higher price probably means that more time and attention has been devoted to its manufacture, that better wood has been used and that all the components are better matched to each other. All this goes to make a better-looking, richer-sounding instrument, that may well be easier — and more fun and more rewarding — to play.

### Better but cheaper

That said, you may very well find a new thousand-dollar instrument that performs and looks better than a new one priced at fifteen hundred dollars, depending, for one thing, on where the instrument was made.

### A good sound for less

The most important tip when you go to buy your first instrument is to take an advanced cellist along. He or she will be able to tell you if a cello sounds much better than its price suggests, or the other way around. If you don't know a cellist you can take along, try asking your teacher. And if you can't find anyone at all, at least buy a cello from someone who plays the instrument.

# STUDENT AND MASTER CELLOS?

All kinds of names are used to classify cellos. What's what, and what do these names mean?

### To begin with...
For example, you may find cellos classified as student, orchestra, and concert instruments. These names seem to suggest that you should start off with the first, buy an orchestra cello once you are good enough to play in an orchestra, and move on to a concert cello as soon as you're ready to play a solo concert… Similarly, there are conservatory and artist cellos.

### Problem
The problem with these names is that everyone has their own ideas about what they mean. For instance, some master violin makers build 'student cellos' that sell for ten times the price of a mass-produced 'concert cello.' So don't pay too much attention to the names. The price of an instrument will usually tell you more.

### Handmade
'Handmade' is another word that can be misleading. Plenty of low-cost production cellos have largely or entirely been built by hand — but that doesn't necessarily mean they're good instruments.

### Master cellos
The term 'master cello' can be just as vague. Officially, though, master cellos are made from start to finish by a master violin maker. They usually cost some ten thousand dollars or more, and you have to be prepared to join a year-long waiting list for delivery. It goes without saying that a master violin maker or luthier does everything by hand — so the word 'handmade' would be redundant in this case.

### Workshop cellos
The term *workshop cello* usually refers to instruments that others may call intermediate or step-up cellos, in the price range of

33

about twelve hundred dollars and more. These are often good, handmade instruments, but they're produced by a team of workers, rather than by one master luthier.

### Old production instruments

Older factory-made cellos can fetch a relatively high price, because many cellists believe that old instruments sound better, or that they're 'the real thing.' Even so, a brand new cello costing twelve hundred dollars may well be a better instrument than an eighteen-hundred-dollar cello that was built in the early 1900s, for example.

### Small cellos

Fractional-sized cellos are not always that much (if any) cheaper than full-sized instruments of the same quality. The same goes for bows, strings, and cases.

TIP

### True story

A true story. A violinist goes to buy an expensive violin. He plays, looks, and listens, plays and listens some more, and then he makes his choice: This violin is the one for him. But he doesn't buy it because, to his shock and surprise, he is told that he picked the cheapest instrument available, priced at only ten thousand dollars — and he was actually looking for an instrument of at least five times that price. Similar stories are told about cellists too ...

# BUYING TIPS

The main buying tip? Try to buy your instrument from people who understand — and love — cellos, as they won't send you home with a barely playable instrument. Also, they will be able to guide you in the sometimes confusing world of the cello, with its numerous brand names and countries of origin. Chapter 14 tells you more about cello brands and makers.

34

## Where to buy?

You can buy cellos in general music stores, which often sell mainly lower-priced production instruments, or from specialized violin dealers and violin makers. Besides expensive handmade (master) cellos, many violin makers supply more affordable instruments too.

## On approval

In some cases you may be able to take an instrument on approval, so that you can assess it at your leisure. This is more common with expensive instruments than with cheap ones, and you are more likely to be offered this opportunity if you are a good cellist than if you are choosing your first instrument.

## Label

You can buy a good cello on the Internet, through a classified ad or at an auction, if you know what to look for. A word of warning, though: There are thousands of cellos around with labels bearing the name Stradivarius, or the name of another famous violin maker. Anyone can make labels. Making cellos or violins is a lot harder.

**Antonio Stradivarius Cremonenfis**
**Faciebat Anno 1999**

## Appraisal

If you find a secondhand instrument anywhere else than at a reputable violin dealer or maker, it's best to have it appraised before you buy. Violin makers can usually tell you exactly what a cello should cost. They'll also tell you anything that's wrong with it, and what it will cost to put it right. An appraisal may cost one or more percent of the value of the cello. If that doesn't amount to much, you may have to pay a minimum charge instead.

## Buying online

You can also buy musical instruments online or by mail-order. This makes it impossible to compare instruments. Online and

35

mail-order companies usually offer a return service for most or all of their products: If you're not happy with your purchase, you can send it back within a certain period of time. Of course the instrument should be in new condition when you send it back.

### Time

Take your time when you go to buy a cello. After all, you want it to last you for a long time. Only if you fall totally in love with an instrument should you buy it straight away. Or perhaps a week or two later, or once you can afford it…

### Fairs and conventions

One last tip: If a string players' or educators' convention is being held in your vicinity, try to attend it. Besides lots of instruments you may be able to try out and compare, you will also come across plenty of product specialists, as well as numerous fellow cellists who are always a good source of information and inspiration.

# MORE AND MORE EXPENSIVE

Professional cellists and conservatory students often play instruments worth tens of thousands of dollars, and there are even cellos that cost two million or more. How do they get so expensive?

### Like paintings

Cellos by Stradivarius, Amati, Guarnerius, and other famous makers of the past don't cost so much only because they're so good, but also because they're some three hundred years old: They're rare, just like the famous great paintings from that era.

### Better?

Though age doesn't necessarily make cellos better, it does make them more expensive. You can easily pay ten times as much — or more — for a high-quality old instrument as for an equally good new one. Even though the sound of a new cello was preferred to that of a famous million-dollar-instrument in blindfold tests more than once, this still doesn't influence the price of the old masters.

> ### Less famous, less expensive
> *The price of an old cello also depends on how well known the maker is. You may be able to buy a very good, rare German cello that's the same age as a Stradivarius for less than twenty thousand dollars.*

**TIP**

### Reasonable?
When discussing old and expensive cellos, you need to watch out with words like good, bad, or reasonable. For every expert who claims that you can get a 'reasonable cello' for some ten thousand dollars, you'll be able to find another expert who will say that 'reasonable' starts at no less than seventy-five grand.

### A few years or fifteen minutes
Likewise, some experts claim that a new cello will start sounding really good only after a few years of playing, while others say it takes fifteen minutes at most; and some experts believe in the use of special vibrating devices that 'break in' your instrument for you, while others don't.

# 5

# A Good Cello

When you first start playing, all cellos seem to look and sound the same. This chapter shows you the differences between them and tells you how to audition them, covering different types of varnishes and wood, cello sizes, tops, backs, bridges, pegs, and all other details of the instrument — as well as its sound, of course.

How a cello sounds depends a lot on how it was built and on the quality of the wood. But the strings are important too, and so is the bow, and the adjustment of the instrument. These three subjects are dealt with in Chapters 6 (*Good Strings*), 7 (*Bows and Rosins*), and 10 (*Cello Maintenance*).

### By ear

The first and major part of this chapter is about everything there is to see on a cello, and what it all means for how the instrument sounds. If you prefer to choose a cello using your ears only, then you can skip ahead to the tips on pages 60–64.

# THE LOOKS

Cellos come in glossy and matte finishes, and some instruments have a warm, satin-like glaze. When it comes to their color, there are even more variations. Some are pale orange or even yellowish, others have a rich amber or a deep brown hue, and still others tend toward red or purple. Cellos in completely different colors, such as green or blue, are very rare — but they are available.

### Oil and spirit

Traditionally, cellos have an oil-based finish, which used to take weeks to dry. Today, these finishes can be dried using ultraviolet light, and you may be able to find oil-varnished cellos for as little as eight hundred dollars. Spirit-based varnishes are used on cellos in most price ranges, often hand-rubbed rather than being sprayed or brushed. Be aware that spirit- and oil-based finishes on inexpensive instruments tend to be quite brittle.

### Invisible repairs

No one finish is typically better than any other. What's really important is that repairs and scratches can be touched up invisibly with both oil-based and spirit-based varnishes. Nitrocellulose lacquer, when applied properly, is a natural, flexible, sprayed-on finish that can be repaired successfully too.

### Synthetic varnishes

Low-priced cellos often have a synthetic finish (i.e., polyurethane). This glossy type of finish can be applied very quickly using spray guns, and it's strong, hard, and easy to clean. Being so hard, on the other hand, it may reduce the instrument's sound potential, especially if it has been applied very thickly. Another drawback is that it doesn't allow for invisible repairs.

### Shading

Cellos are not always the same color all over. Older instruments may have a lighter patch where the left hand touches the body, for instance. These worn-out patches are sometimes imitated on new cellos. This technique, *shading*, makes instruments look older than they really are.

### Checked finish

Older cellos often have a *checked finish*, the varnish being marked with a web of tiny cracks. This effect, also known as *craquelure*, can be imitated by the maker too. Yet another way to make an instrument look older is to bring out the grain by applying a dark dye.

### Aged to order

*Antiquing* is a generic name for making a cello look older than it is, which often raises its price. If you have an instrument custom-built, you can of course ask to have it 'antiqued.' Even minor damage and worn-out patches can be imitated. These aging processes are purely cosmetic.

### Flamed wood

The wood of the backs and *ribs* (sides) of many cellos looks like it's been licked by flames. This flamed, figured, or curled wood is common on more expensive instruments, but you may also find it in the lowest price range. Whether the wood is plain, or slightly-, medium-, or well-flamed does not relate to its quality or sound potential.

On the other hand, beautifully flamed wood has its price: In student and intermediate price ranges the highly-flamed instruments are often the most expensive ones.

41

*A mirrored, flamed back.*

### Bookmatched

Many flamed backs clearly show that they're made up of two precisely mirrored or *bookmatched* halves (see page 152).

### The volute

Something else to look at is the volute, which usually has three windings. The center (the *ears*) can stick out more or less, and volutes are also different when it comes to the *fluting* — the carved grooves in the back. The scroll is sometimes referred to as the signature of the instrument: Experts can tell the maker of a master cello by simply looking at the scroll.

*The volute is one of the maker's signatures.*

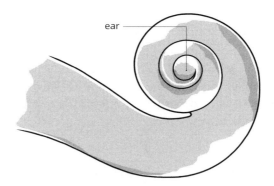

ear

### Purfling

The inlaid purfling is not just for decoration. It also prevents cracks at the edge from extending to the *plates* (top and back). Double purfling, a characteristic of the Brescian school (see page 158) is rare, but you may come across it. A tip: On very cheap cellos, the purfling is sometimes not inlaid, but painted, or scratched into the wood and dyed.

42

single purfling         double purfling

*Purfling usually consists of three or more inlaid strips of wood.*

# THE BODY

Generally speaking, a larger body will give you a slightly larger sound. Some instruments have noticeably wider bodies, or just a wider or a slimmer waist (the *C-bout*), and some cellos are slightly shorter or taller than others.

### The ribs

Cellos may vary in their depth too. A relatively shallow instrument (with low *ribs*) may sound a little thin; a cello that is too deep may have a hollow sound. A cello is always a little deeper at the tail than it is at the top of the body.

### String length

If you measure the *string length* (from the nut to the bridge) of a number of instruments you may find differences too. The usual string length is 27.36" (695 mm).

When trying out a number of instruments, you may find yourself playing out of tune on some of them. This may be due to a different string length, or to a different *mensur ratio*. More about this can be found in the Glossary (*String length*, page 189). Learning to play an instrument with deviant dimensions in tune usually takes just a little time.

43

### The top

*The top is the main part of a cello. When you play, the strings make the top vibrate, and it is mainly these vibrations that determine the sound of the instrument. This is why the top is often referred to as the soundboard.*

### Spruce and maple

The top, also known as *table* or *belly*, is almost always made of solid spruce, which has been carved into shape. Spruce is also used for the bass bar and the sound post. The back is usually made of one or two carved pieces of solid maple, a heavier and denser type of wood. Maple is used for the ribs and the neck as well. One-piece backs are often made of other types of wood, such as willow or poplar, both softer woods, resulting in a slightly softer, warmer sound.

### Laminated wood

Cheap cellos may have a laminated back or top, or both. These plywood plates are very durable and crack-resistant, but they will not make for a rich, musical sound. If you're not sure whether the plates are solid or plywood, check the edges of the plates and the *f*-holes.

### Fine grain

Cellists often prefer the top to have a grain that is straight, even, and not too wide, getting gradually finer toward the center of the instrument.
Of course, some cellos have a beautiful grain but don't sound good, and there are great instruments with a wide, uneven, or wavy grain as well.

### The arching

A top with a lower *arching* will usually help produce a stronger, more powerful and direct sound; a higher arching may contribute to a softer, warmer timbre. Most modern cello tops are slightly over an inch high. The back is usually a little flatter.

44

*The back is a little flatter than the top.*

### The channel

A cello with a deep, broad channel will often have a softer sound than an instrument that has only a hint of this 'valley' along the edge.

**TIP**

### Flowing lines

*You can spend hours looking at cello archings. They all look similar, yet they're all slightly different. What is especially important is that the lines of the arch flow, that there are no flat parts or odd angles, and that the arching isn't too high, too low, or too narrow. The more often you look, the more you will see.*

### Thick and thin

Low-cost cellos may have thicker tops or backs, which are easier to make. If they're too thick, the instrument may sound thinnish. Good instruments have *graduated* plates, their exact thickness varying from spot to spot. The top usually varies from about 0.19" in the middle to 0.14" at the edges (4.75–3.5 mm). The back is a little thicker overall.

### Hot hide glue

Most better instruments are assembled using animal glue (*hot hide glue*). Joints fixed with this type of glue can be loosened, for example to take the top off for repairs inside the instrument. Also, this type of glue will let go if the wood shrinks or expands as a result of age, or changes in humidity, for instance when winter

**45**

comes. This prevents the plates from cracking; all the violin maker has to do is to apply new glue. The overhang of the edges warrants that these 'repairs' can be made invisible.

### Carbon fiber cellos

Various companies make carbon fiber cellos. These instruments are extremely durable and require less maintenance than wooden instruments.

# NECK AND FINGERBOARD

The neck and fingerboard affect not only the playability, but also the sound of a cello.

### Ebony

Fingerboards are almost always made of ebony. This is a nearly black, extremely hard type of wood. The smoother and more even the fingerboard, the more easily it plays. Cheap cellos sometimes have fingerboards of softer, light-colored wood, which is often dyed black to make it look like ebony. You can sometimes recognize such fingerboards by lighter patches or pale spots on the sides.

### Wear

After years of use, even the hardest fingerboard will wear, after which it should be reworked or, eventually, replaced (see Chapter 10, *Cello Maintenance*). Incidentally, the use of ebony doesn't guarantee a good fingerboard per se: There are cheap, soft types of ebony as well.

### Clearance

The fingerboard has a curved top, similar to the top of the bridge. On most fingerboards, the area under the C-string has been flattened. This provides extra clearance for the wide vibrations of this string, preventing it from rattling against the fingerboard. These fingerboards, introduced by the German cellist Bernard

46

Romberg in the mid-nineteenth century, are recognizable by the sharp 'ridge' between the G- and the C-string.

### Thick fingers

The grooves in the nut, at the top of the fingerboard, determine the string spacing and the string height at that end. Nuts can be replaced to adjust both string spacing and height. For example, if you have thick fingers, you may prefer a nut with grooves set a little further apart.

nut

*The nut can be replaced.*

### Feel the neck

Necks are always much lighter in color: A dark neck would soon show worn patches. On more expensive cellos, the wood is usually not varnished but protected with an oil finish. Two tips:

- Feel if the curve of the neck lies nicely in your hand and **check the neck** for odd pits or bumps.

- Necks differ in how thick they are. A **thicker neck feels differently** from a thinner neck.

### Concave fingerboard

The fingerboard is very slightly concave along its length. This prevents the strings from buzzing when playing in the higher positions.

### Straight

The neck and fingerboard, from scroll to body, should of course be straight. They should also be set exactly in the center line of the

47

*The fingerboard: slightly concave.*

cello, and they shouldn't look as though someone has tried to wrench the instrument out of shape. To check, just take a good long look along the fingerboard from the scroll toward the bridge. Also check whether the strings run perfectly straight along the fingerboard, which of course requires a properly installed tailpiece and bridge.

### Neck angle

The neck of a modern cello is tilted slightly backwards. Before the 1800s, there was a 90-degree angle between the neck and the side of the body. These instruments sounded softer, as the larger neck angle reduced the pressure of the strings on the bridge. Conversely, a smaller neck angle means more pressure on the bridge, which makes the sound bigger, louder, or more radiant.

*A smaller neck angle gives a bigger sound.*

neck angle

**TIP**

### Baroque cello

*A larger neck angle is characteristic of the Baroque cello, which is still used to play music of the Baroque era (c. 1600–1750). The instrument's mellow, gentle sound is also due to a lower bridge, a shorter neck, the use of gut strings, a different bow, and a lower tuning.*

48

# STRING HEIGHT

The string height is the distance between the strings and the fingerboard. If your strings are too high above the fingerboard, playing will be hard work. If they are too low, they may rattle. In between, it's largely a matter of taste and the type of strings you're using. A greater string height can give your instrument a slightly clearer, brighter, or more powerful sound.

### Room to move

At the nut, the strings are very close to the fingerboard. At the other end, the distance between the fingerboard and the strings is a lot bigger. The thick strings are always slightly higher above the fingerboard than the thin ones, because they need more room to move.

### The figures

As a rule of thumb, if you use steel core strings, the A-string should be about 0.18"–0.22" (4.5–5.5 mm) above the end of the fingerboard, and the C-string about 0.26"–0.30" (6.5–7.5 mm). Add about 0.04" (1 mm) for gut strings, and about 0.02" for synthetic core strings.

### Too high

If you have a new cello that has not yet been properly adjusted, the strings will probably be too high. Adjusting may involve having the bridge and the nut adapted.

# THE BRIDGE

The bridge influences both string height and the sound or timbre of the instrument.

### Straight

Bridges are a bit slanted at the front and straight at the back. The

49

straight back should be perpendicular to the instrument's top, and the middle of the bridge's feet should be located exactly between the notches of the f-holes. However, some instruments sound better if the bridge is moved forward or backward a tiny bit – so a bridge may also be located on a line between the two lower (inner) notches, for example.

*... exactly between the notches of the f-holes...*

### Flecked

Some bridges are plain, while others may be highly flecked or speckled. In itself, this difference tells you nothing about the quality of the wood: Non-flecked (plain), slightly flecked, and highly flecked wood is used for both cheap and expensive bridges. A fine, straight grain is more important.

*A flecked bridge: cheap or expensive...*

### (Un)treated

String instrument catalogs often indicate whether bridges are treated or untreated, which refers to the bridges being finished with varnish or oil. Some makers feel that this finish enhances the quality of the bridge; others prefer untreated ones.

### Too heavy, too light

Of course you're not going to weigh the bridge when you're choosing a cello, but it's worth knowing that a heavy bridge can muffle the sound slightly, just like a mute (see page 96). A vèry light bridge may be the culprit if an instrument has a thin, weak, or uncentered tone. The hardness of the wood also plays a role. A bridge made of harder wood helps produce more volume and a stronger, brighter tone.

### French and Belgian bridges

Cello bridges come in two basic models. The French type of bridge has shorter legs and longer wings; Belgian bridges, with longer legs, have less mass. Soundwise, French bridges enhance the lower frequencies of the instrument, and they may make the sound a bit mellower. Conversely, you may want to use a Belgian bridge for a brighter, more pronounced sound and a lot of clarity on the D- and A-strings, but the low register may suffer a little.

A French (left) and a Belgian bridge (right).

### Blanks

The bridges you find in stores and catalogs are blanks: Bridges always need to be custom-fit to your instrument. There are bridges with moveable feet that automatically adjust to the arch of the top

51

— but even if you prefer this type of bridge, it should be installed by a specialist: Properly fitting a bridge to an instrument involves more than carving the feet (see also page 128).

### Too deep

Eventually, the strings will wear into the bridge. If the grooves have become too deep, the strings will be muffled and harder to tune. The string height will be decreased as well, and the strings may break sooner. Ideally, the grooves should be just so deep that two-thirds of the thickness of each string sticks out above the bridge.

### Cutting string

The thin A-string is the one most likely to cut into your bridge. This can be prevented by a plastic sleeve (see page 75) or a piece of vellum (parchment) under the string. Some bridges have a bone or hardwood insert for the same purpose.

*A bridge with an ebony inset.*

### Two at once

The top of the bridge has almost the same curve as the fingerboard. Beginning cellists often prefer a highly-curved bridge: A higher curve reduces the chance of inadvertently bowing two strings instead of one.

### Warping bridges

Nearly all bridges warp slightly in time with the pressure of the strings. A cello will produce its best sound only with a straight bridge — so check your bridge from time to time (also see page 127).

> ### Height and tone
> *The bridge height influences both string height and tone.*
> *A slightly higher bridge increases the string tension, which*
> *makes the sound a little brighter or stronger. If the bridge is*
> *too high, the sound may become a little hollow.*

**TIP**

# THE SOUND POST

Inside the body, slightly 'behind' the bridge, is the sound post. This thin spruce rod and its placement are essential for the sound of your cello. French violin makers even call it *l'âme*: the *soul* of the instrument.

### Position
The sound post must be straight, and long enough to be firmly wedged, but not so long that it pushes the top and the back apart. The exact position is critical too.

### Adjustment
A violin maker can adjust the timbre of a cello by moving the sound post a fraction. This way the sound can be made slightly less edgy, or a little brighter, for example. Also, if one string sounds louder or softer than the others, the violin maker can do something about it by repositioning the sound post. You can also try using different strings — but that's another chapter (Chapter 6, to be precise).

# PEGS AND FINE TUNERS

To tune a cello, you use the wooden tuning pegs at the top of the instrument. If you play steel strings, you will have to use the fine tuners in the tailpiece as well. Both pegs and fine tuners come in different types and sizes.

53

### Ebony, rosewood, boxwood

Tuning pegs get thicker toward the thumb piece. This tapered shape prevents them from slipping. They are usually made of ebony, which is also used for fingerboards and tailpieces. Rosewood and boxwood are popular too. Rosewood has a reddish-brown color; boxwood is usually yellowish.

### Worn grooves

If the wood of the pegs is too soft, the strings will soon wear grooves into them. These grooves, in turn, may damage the strings.

### A good fit

Cheap cellos are often hard to tune, or they go out of tune quickly because the pegs are poor in quality or haven't been custom-fit to the instrument properly.

### Parisian eyes

Pegs come with various peg head designs, a familiar one being an inverted heart with a ball on top. Another type of decoration is a *Parisian eye*: a small, mother-of-pearl dot with a metal ring around it. A single mother-of-pearl dot is called a (*single*) *eye* or *eyelet*.

### Removable pegs

Depending on your posture and the way you hold the cello, the

*Various tuning-peg designs.*

basic peg     Parisian eye     ball     inverted heart

54

tuning pegs of the C- and G-strings may bother you. To solve that problem, you can have your instrument provided with tuning pegs with a removable thumb piece. Once your strings have been tuned, you simply take out the 'keys.'

### Fine tuners

Steel core strings respond so quickly to turning the big tuning pegs that you need fine tuners to get them at their exact pitches. Usually, these fine tuners are built into the tailpiece. They're also known as *adjusters, tuning adjusters, string adjusters, string tuners...*

**Tipcode CELLO-006**
This short video demonstrates the use of a fine tuner.

**TIPCODE**

### Too heavy

You can buy fine tuners separately as well, usually at some ten dollars each. A tip: If your cello has a wooden tailpiece, which usually is quite heavy by itself, the added weight of the fine tuners may muffle the sound of your instrument. If so, you may be better off buying a lightweight alloy or synthetic tailpiece with built-in fine tuners.

### Geared pegs

Instead of fine tuners, you can get a special type of pegs with a built-in planetary gear system. These 'gear boxes' allow for both rough and fine tuning. Also, these special pegs are easier to operate than traditional pegs, and they don't stick or slip with changes in temperature and humidity.

**TIP**

**55**

## Metal pegs and tuning machines

As a rarely used alternative there are metal pegs with very thin shafts. Also, some (mainly older) cellos have metal tuning machines similar to the ones used on double basses.

# TAILPIECE

Tailpieces, believe it or not, may also influence the sound of your instrument — though you need to have a good instrument and be a good cellist to notice those subtleties. Tailpieces come in various materials and designs, and with or without decoration or built-in fine tuners.

### French or Hill

There is a great variety of tailpiece models available. Two examples of well-known basic designs would be the French model, with a very slim upper section, or the Hill model, named after a British manufacturer, with elegant lines and an angular end. Some tailpieces have a Parisian eye or other inlaid decorations.

### Parallel

The strings should always run parallel between the bridge and the

56

A French
model
tailpiece...

tailpiece saddle

... and a Hill
tailpiece.

tailpiece. If not, the tailpiece may be too narrow or too wide for the instrument.

### The sound
The tailpiece has roughly the same effect on the sound of the cello as the bridge. A heavy, wooden tailpiece can slightly muffle the sound, making it a little less bright, somewhat similar to what a heavy bridge or a light mute would do. Conversely, a lighter (alloy or synthetic) tailpiece promotes a clearer, brighter sound. The sound may become a bit uncentered too. A light-weight bridge may have that same effect.

### All together
Of course, these differences are not that obvious. However, the combined mass of a heavy, wooden tailpiece with four big fine tuners can make your instrument sound noticeably duller, especially if the tailpiece is too close to the bridge (see page 129).

### Tailpiece loop
Traditionally, the tailpiece loop or *hanger* is made of gut, hence its other name, *tailgut*. Some cellists prefer real gut as they

57

believe this enhances the sound of the instrument. Gut may also contribute to the looks of older instruments. However, most tailpieces are attached with an adjustable synthetic cord, which is more reliable and cheaper, or with a steel wire.

*Tailpiece with adjustable loop and built-in fine tuners.*

## END PIN

The end pin doesn't do much more than support the instrument. To prevent the height adjustment thumb screw from slipping, the rod may have indentations or a knurled surface. A tip: If the rod has indentations, you may use them to memorize its height setting.

### Collar
A cello with a full ebony trim also has an ebony end pin plug, but plugs can be made of other types of wood too. Some have decorations, such as a gold-plated collar around the plug.

*Two different end-pin designs.*

plug or button

adjustment screw

rod

rubber tip

### Hollow or solid

End pins come with a hollow or a solid rod, the latter simply being a little heavier. Most experts agree that the end pin does not influence the tone of the instrument. However, some players prefer hollow (or solid) rods for sound reasons. Similarly, some favor wooden end pins, which have become quite rare, and others use a modern, light-weight carbon fiber version.

### Comparing end pins

Comparing end pins with your ears is usually quite hard, by the way — first, because the differences are so subtle, and second, because replacing them is not simply a matter of pulling one out and putting another one in.

_TIP_

### Bent end pin

_Players who prefer playing with their instrument in a more prone position may benefit from a bent, or angled, endpin. On some end pins you can even adjust the angle._

### Rubber tip

The rubber tip at the end of the rod won't keep the instrument from slipping away on all surfaces. If you take the tip off, you will usually see a sharp steel point, which works even better on most wooden surfaces — but of course, you're not supposed to damage the floor you're playing on.

### Anchors

To prevent your instrument from sliding away or from damaging the floor or a rug, you may use an end pin anchor. These are available in a wide variety, ranging from simple rubber balls and non-skid discs to holders that can be attached to the front legs of your chair with adjustable straps or cords. They usually cost between ten and twenty-five dollars. The designs that attach to your chair are guaranteed to work on all surfaces. Some players feel that the sound suffers from using an end pin holder; they

59

prefer playing with the steel point stuck into a wooden stage. Other experts state that no one can tell the difference.

### Height setting
The best height setting for the end pin depends on many factors, from your height and your posture, to the height of your seat, and the angle at which you hold the cello. Most rods are adjustable up to 20", and they can be replaced by even longer ones.

### Cello chairs
Children need a lower seat for optimum posture. Special height-adjustable cello chairs are available, but other height-adjustable chairs and stools may do also — as long as they have a flat or slightly forward-leaning seat. Some players prefer a saddle-shaped seat.

# AUDITIONING CELLOS

If you try ten cellos in a row, you'll have forgotten what the first one sounded like by the time you try the last. Here are some tips for auditioning or play-testing instruments.

### Take it with you
If you already have a cello, take it with you when you go to choose a new one. Comparing it to different cellos makes it easier to judge what you hear. If you have your own bow, take that with you too. Otherwise, use the best bow available in the store. Using a good bow will give you a better idea of what the different cellos are capable of.

### Someone else
If you don't play yourself, or have only just started, you won't know whether an instrument has a poor sound, or whether it's just you. So ask someone who knows how to play the instrument to demonstrate the different cellos for you: the sales person for example, or your teacher.

60

### By ear

If you ask someone else to play, you can also hear how the instrument sounds from a distance. That sound will be quite different compared to having it right by your ear. Another tip: If you simply can't choose between a few cellos, turn around. Then you won't know which one is being played, so you'll really be choosing by ear only.

You won't see the price, the finish, the brand name, or the age anymore. Sometimes musicians choose much cheaper instruments than they expected to by ear — but it may be the other way around too.

### Very different

To get an idea of how cellos sound in the room you're in, you may start by playing two very different cellos, one with a bright sound, and one with a mellow, dark sound. Knowing these extremes also can make your search easier.

### Three by three

First, make a rough selection of the instruments you like on first hearing. Take three of them, and compare them with one another. Replace the one you like least by another cello from your rough selection. Compare the three again — and so on.

### Something simple

If you have a lot of cellos to choose from, it's often best to just play briefly on each one. Play something simple, so that you can concentrate on what you hear, rather than on what you play. Even a scale will do. When you have a few cellos left, and you really need to choose, you'll probably want to play longer and more demanding pieces so that you can get to know the instruments better.

### String by string

You can also compare cellos string by string and note by note. How do the open strings sound, and how do they sound in the highest positions? Is there a good balance between the volume of the strings in all positions? How do the strings sound when you pluck them, or when you play long notes?

61

TIP

> ### Same pitch, same strings
>
> *The cellos that you are comparing must be tuned properly and to the same pitch. Otherwise, one instrument might sound a little warmer than the others, say, just because it is tuned a bit lower. For similar reasons, the cellos you are judging should all have the same or similar strings. If not, you will be comparing strings instead of cellos.*

# LISTENING TO CELLOS

Here are some things to listen for when auditioning cellos.

### Projection and volume

Some cellos just sound very soft or weak, however energetically you play them. If you play such an instrument in an orchestra, no one will be able to hear you. Other cellos can be heard at a fair distance too, even if you play very softly. A cello like that has good projection. Of course, cellos also differ in the volume level they can produce: Some just sound louder than others.

### Same note, different timbre

The A-string not only sounds higher than the other strings, it also sounds different. If you first play an A on the open A-string, and then play the same pitch on the D- and G-strings, you'll hear that very same pitch with three very different timbres.

Cellists usually want their low strings to sound warm and dark, and their higher strings to sound brilliant and sing brightly, all within a musical balance: The differences from string to string should not be like going from one instrument to another.

### Response and depth of sound

A cello should have a good response, even when you play very softly. If not, the instrument will be hard to play; it will make you really work for each note. If a cello has a poor response, it takes a little while before the tone is really 'there.' The C-string is the most critical one when it comes to response, as it's so heavy. This string is also most likely to lack depth of sound, followed by its neighbor, the G.

_TIP_

### Uncentered tone

*On some cellos, the sound never seems to gel; these instruments lack foundation, producing an uncentered, weak tone. Both a slow response and an uncentered tone can also stem from the strings, the bow, the rosin, or — sadly — yourself.*

### Dynamics and colors

A cello should be able to sound just as loud or as soft as you play. If it does, it has good dynamics. If it doesn't, your performance will always be a bit shallow. The instrument should also allow you to produce different timbres or 'colors.' One example: If you play a little closer to the fingerboard, the sound is supposed to become noticeably rounder than if you play close to the bridge (*sul ponticello*). Ideally, the instrument should sound good both ways, leaving you plenty of room to color the sound.

### Sound and words

Apart from that, sound is mostly a matter of personal preference. Bear in mind that when two people listen to the same instrument, they'll probably use different words to describe what they hear. What one finds harsh or edgy (in other words, unpleasant), another may describe as bright and clear (in other words, pleasant), and what's warm to one ear sounds dull to another. It all depends on what you do and do not like, and how you put that into words.

### Poor

Some words associated with poorer-sounding instruments are nasal (as if it has a cold), hollow (like you're playing in a bathroom), thin (as if it were a miniature instrument), or dull (as if there were a blanket over it) — and everybody has more or less the same idea of what those words mean.

**63**

### Rich

The better an instrument is, the richer it sounds. Richer means a beautiful, resonant, full-throated tone; it means there's more of everything; and it means that the cello allows for producing a wide variety of tonal colors: mellow and vivid, subdued and bright, sad and happy…

## USED CELLOS

When you go to buy a used instrument, there are a few extra things you should remember.

### Repairs

No matter what's broken, a decent cello can almost always be fixed. Of course, if you decide to buy an instrument that needs some work, you need to know what it's going to cost first. Some types of damage are easy to see, other kinds only an expert will spot. Also, you need to be an expert to judge things like how well a cello has been repaired. If in doubt, take a cello for appraisal first (see also page 35).

*Major damage: cracks in the sound post and bass bar areas.*

### Checking out used instrument

Here are some things to check when buying a secondhand instrument. A complete list would be too long for this book.

- **Varnish wears**. One place to check is where your left hand touches the body. If the varnish has completely gone, you may need to have something done about it.

- If the type of varnish allows for it, it is usually **touched up** after repairs (see page 40). See if this has been done properly.

- Check **the edges**: This is where the instruments gets bumped most often. Repairing damaged edges can cost a lot of money.

- **Cracks** in the top or the back always run lengthwise. Cracks by the sound post and the bass bar are often hard to see and even harder to repair.

- Other places to check for cracks include the **neck base and the cheeks** (sides) of the pegbox near the pegs.

*Cracks in the cheeks and the neck base.*

---

### Woodworm

*Woodworm burrows into wood and leaves narrow tunnels. This can be very serious, especially if it has been at work in the top or the back. You won't find woodworm in a cello that has always been played: This particular animal doesn't like music. If you want to know whether it's still around, lay the instrument on a piece of black cardboard overnight. If there's sawdust on the cardboard the next day, the cello has tenants.*

**TIP**

65

- If the **tuning pegs** are pushed very far into the pegbox, sticking way out at the other end, they may need to be replaced, and the holes may need to be rebushed. This is quite expensive.

- Glue can come loose, along the edges for instance, or at the neck. To discover **loose glue joints** you can play the instrument or gently tap it, all around the body.

# 6

# Good Strings

*The strings you use determine your sound to a great extent. You can choose between dozens of different types of strings, with different core materials and windings. Every type of string has its own timbre, some types of strings are easier to play than others, and some sound better on one cello than on another.*

Cello strings can last a long time — up to a year, or even longer. It does help if they are fitted properly and kept clean. For more information on replacing strings and keeping them in good condition, go to Chapter 10, *Cello Maintenance*.

### Steel, gut, synthetic

There are three main types of strings. Today, most cellists use strings with a steel core. Originally, cellos had gut strings, which sound a lot warmer and darker. Strings with a synthetic core — the third type — have a sound in between the other two.

### Winding

Almost all cello strings are wound with ultra-thin metal ribbon. If not, they would have to be very thick in order to produce the desired pitches — and thick strings do not respond very well. The material of the ribbon is very important to the way the strings sound, play, and respond.

*... wound with ultra-thin metal ribbon.*

### Important

Strings are very important for how you sound and play. Actually, the difference between using cheap and expensive strings is often much bigger than the difference between a cheaper and a more expensive cello.

### Experiment

So, if you can afford it, try to experiment with different types of strings. When you do, please note that changing from steel to synthetic or gut strings will require you to adapt your technique, which may require extra lessons from a teacher who plays those types of strings. Your instrument will probably need to be adapted too (see page 126).

68

# STEEL STRINGS

Strings with a steel core offer a clear, bright, powerful sound and an immediate response. Also, they're very reliable and they last a long time, typically from six months to a year, or even longer.

### The core
Steel strings come in two basic variations: with a solid core, and with a core made up of a number of very thin steel strands. *Solid-core* or *full-core strings* have the brightest sound. *Multi-strand* or *spiral-core strings* are more flexible, and produce a darker, fuller tone.

### Combinations
Many cellists combine both types on their instrument. They often use solid-core A- and D-strings for radiant, bright highs, and multi-strand G- and C-strings for warm, full-sounding lows. Others combine synthetic and steel strings, for example choosing synthetic C- and G-strings, and steel strings for the D and the A. Such 'custom sets' are readily available from various cello string companies, but you can make up your own combination as well, of course.

### The price
Most cheap cellos have steel strings, as they are relatively low-priced. A set of four is available for around seventy-five dollars, and sometimes even less. Professional-quality steel strings may easily cost twice as much, and there are C-strings that list for more than a hundred dollars.

# GUT STRINGS

The first cellos had sheep gut strings. Many professional musicians still feel that this is the only type of string that can really reveal the instrument's beauty.

69

### Sound

The sound of gut strings is often described as mellow, warm, and rich. They allow for great variation in color and inflection — which in turn demands a good cellist, and a good cello too. Baroque music (see page 84), requiring a warm, gentle type of sound, is often played using gut strings. These are sometimes wound with round wire (round wound), like in the Baroque era, rather than with a flat ribbon. Some Baroque players use unwound (plain) D- and A-strings.

### A few hours

Contrary to steel strings, gut strings need to be broken in: It takes a few hours of playing to get them to develop their full sound. As they stretch a fair bit when new, you'll have to tune gut strings quite often at first. Additional tuning is also required as gut strings detune with changes in temperature or humidity.

### Expensive

A set of gut strings easily costs a hundred to two hundred dollars, but they're available for less as well. What adds to their price is that they don't last as long as other types of strings. Many cellists use a gut A-string only, combined with three synthetic-core strings.

## SYNTHETIC STRINGS

Synthetic-core strings could be considered 'in between' gut and steel, in terms of sound, life expectancy, and price. A set of four typically costs a hundred dollars or more.

### Sound

As there's a large variety in synthetic-core materials and windings, there's a large variety in sound too. Generally speaking, the sound is close to that of gut strings, though a bit brighter and louder. Synthetic strings are more reliable and less expensive, and they last longer. Compared to steel strings they sound noticeably warmer — or less hard and bright...

### Best of both worlds

Synthetic-core strings are often combined with other types of strings. One popular combination is to use synthetic-core strings for the C and the G, and steel for the other two.

### Breaking them in

Just like gut strings, synthetic-core strings may start to sound their best only after they have been played for a few hours. When they are brand-new, they can sound a little raw or harsh. Also, they're a bit stretchy when new, so they will require additional tuning, and a bit of time to settle in.

# WINDINGS

String manufacturers use various types of windings, each with its own effect on the strings' sound and playability. To create a particular balance between the four strings, they may even use different winding materials within one set, and individual strings can also have more than one winding.

### Nickel or chrome

Generally speaking, a nickel winding will make for a rather soft, sweet, or warm sound. Chromium or chrome-alloy windings, on the other hand, promote a brighter sound and help enhance the projection of the instrument.

### Silver, aluminum, and tungsten

A silver winding adds warmth and power to the lower strings. Silver-wound lower strings are often combined with aluminum-wound treble strings, the lighter metal providing extra clarity in the higher ranges.

Tungsten is used instead of or in combination with silver. This dense material allows for even thinner low strings, which enhances their response. Tungsten may also help to fight wolf tones (see page 99).

71

### More

There are many more materials used to wind strings, including copper, titanium, and silver mixed with gold.

If you are looking for a particular sound, a good salesperson or violin maker will be able to help you with your choice. But if you want to be really sure, you'll need to try out different strings for yourself.

### Discolor

Depending on your perspiration and chemical makeup, silver and aluminum windings may discolor very fast. If this happens, the best you can do is experiment with other types of windings.

## LOUD OR SOFT

Synthetic and steel strings often come in several varieties: *dolce* (soft), *medium*, and *forte* (strong), for instance. You may also see German descriptions such as *weich* (soft) and *stark* (strong). Forte strings, also indicated as *orchestra* or *solo*, are heavier than dolce strings.

### Different tensions

Some string manufacturers describe their strings by their tension, marketing low-, medium-, and high-tension strings. The higher the tension, the heavier the string's gauge. High-tension strings take a little more effort to play and they respond slower than low-tension versions, but their brighter, stronger sound enhances the projection of your instrument. Medium strings are the most commonly used. Low-tension strings are often recommended for old instruments.

### Too much

Choosing the right type of strings is not just down to the sound or playability: Using forte strings may work great on one cello, but their higher tension may actually reduce the sound on another instrument.

## Colors

To indicate the different types of strings, manufacturers use colored thread at one of the string's ends. At the other end, the string's pitch is marked with another color, to prevent you from putting the D-string where the A-string should be, for example.

## Confusing

Unfortunately, these color codes are not standardized, so the same color may mean one thing for one make and something else for the next. Likewise, there's no consistency in what (string type, string pitch) is indicated at which end of the string. Confusing…

## Same make and series

A tip: If the strings on a cello are of the same make and series, you will see four different colors (indicating the pitch of each string) at one end, and only one color (indicating the series or type of strings) at the other.

## Mixed up

If this is not so, there's a fair chance that the strings are of different brands, series, or tensions — combined either on purpose or inadvertently. If the strings sound good together, that's no problem. If you want to know which strings are fitted on your instrument, ask an expert, who can tell from the color codes.

## Thick or thin

Gut strings come in different gauges. Heavier-gauge strings take more effort to play. They sound noticeably fuller, louder, and clearer, but they don't respond as easily as thinner strings.

### String height

If you fit higher-tension strings on your instrument, those strings may end up further from the fingerboard. Conversely, lower-tension strings can decrease the instrument's string height, as they reduce the tension on the neck. Adjusting string height is a job for a professional.

73

### Inches and millimeters

If you want to know exactly how thick a gut string is in inches, divide its gauge by 500 (e.g., a 14 is 14÷500 = 0.028"). To get millimeters, divide the gauge by 20.

# AND MORE

If you're putting new strings on your cello, you can list their details on page 199 of this book. Then you'll be able to buy the same type again if you like them, or avoid them if you don't. This can be especially helpful if you mix and match string sets yourself. The more you know about the strings you use, the better you'll be able to adjust the sound of your instrument to your taste.

### How long

How long cello strings last depends on many things — on how often you play, of course, but also on the core material of the strings and the type of winding, and on how well you maintain your strings (see Chapter 10, *Cello Maintenance*). A tip: If the tension on a string is suddenly released (for example, because of an ill-fitting tuning peg or a sudden change in air humidity; see pages 130–132), the winding may be damaged or the string may break as you bring it back to pitch.

### A year

If you have steel strings and you play for a few hours a week,

TIP

> ## Short and dull
>
> When should you replace your strings? When plucking them only produces a short, dull tone, they are wearing out. Tarnish is another sign that you may have to change your strings. Note, however, that silver-wound and aluminum-wound strings may still sound fine long after they have begun to change color.

you might try fitting new strings after a year or so. If you hear the difference straightaway, try replacing the new set a couple of months earlier. If you can't hear any difference after a year, you may wait longer before replacing your strings next time. Steel strings usually last longer then synthetic strings. Gut strings wear out the quickest.

### Damaged windings

A damaged winding often renders a string unplayable. You can prevent this from happening by making sure the grooves in the bridge and nut are wide enough for the strings you use (have them checked when you change to thicker strings), and by 'lubricating' the grooves from time to time by rubbing them with a soft lead pencil point.

### Sleeves

Some strings come with short sleeves that are designed to protect the winding at the bridge. If you choose to use them, make sure that most of the sleeve is on the side of the tailpiece; otherwise it will muffle the sound too much. If muffling an overly bright string is what you want to do, there are more effective devices available (see pages 96–98).

### Parchment

To prevent the thin A-string from cutting into the bridge, some bridges have an ebony or bone insert at that point, and violin makers often glue a tiny piece of vellum (parchment) under the string.

### Fractional sizes

Fractional-sized strings are available for smaller instruments. Regular strings will typically provide insufficient tension, resulting in a weak tone and possible string breakage. The choice in fractional-sized strings is quite limited; it's usually best to rely on the teacher's experience in this matter. Incidentally, some teachers happen to prefer certain types of regular strings on small cellos.

### String brands

Choosing the right strings can also be hard because of the wide selection that is available. There are quite a number of string

75

brands on the market. Most of them offer various types of cello strings, and some market rosins and other accessories as well. D'Addario, Pirastro, Super-Sensitive, and Thomastik are some of the bigger companies. Other brands are Corelli, Jargar, Larsen, and Dogal, Meisel, Pinnacle, Prim, Pyramid, Savarez, Stellar, Supreme, and Syntha-Core. Some of these names are brand names only, their strings being produced by another company.

# 7

# **Bows and Rosins**

You'll only get the very best from your cello if you have a bow that suits your instrument as well as your style of playing and the music you play. A chapter about brazilwood and pernambuco, synthetic bows, frogs, ferrules, horsehair or synthetic hair, weight and balance, and rosin.

The stick of the bow can be made of wood or a synthetic material, with wood still being the most popular choice. Most cheaper wooden bows have a brazilwood stick; more expensive bows usually feature a pernambuco stick.

### Brazil or pernambuco

Expect to pay two to four hundred dollars for a decent brazilwood bow — but they're available for much less too. If you pay more, you'll probably get a bow with a stick made of pernambuco, a slightly reddish type of wood. Pernambuco bows can last more than a hundred years without losing their elasticity.

### Four hundred

So, for around four hundred dollars you can buy an 'expensive' brazilwood bow or an affordable pernambuco one. If two bows cost the same, choose the one that suits you and your instrument best — whichever type of wood the bow is made of. Snakewood, a dense, expensive type of wood that derives its name from its snakeskin look, is mainly used for special Baroque bows.

### Synthetic bows

Some bows have a synthetic stick — carbon fiber or fiberglass, for example. The cheapest models, available for fifty dollars or less, are designed mainly for children. They're very durable and don't need much care or attention. Professional synthetic bows are also available, and they can cost thousands of dollars.

### Synthetic hair

The very cheapest bows often come with synthetic hair. This provides less grip than the traditional horsehair, and it'll never make the instrument sound its best.

TIP

## Bleaching

*Some manufacturers bleach the bow hair to make it look bright and white all over. However, bleaching reduces the durability of the hair.*

### The mountings

A bow's *mountings* are its metal parts, such as the screw button, the *back plate* of the frog, and the *ferrule* or *D-ring*, where the bow hair enters the frog. The material used for the mounting very roughly indicates the price range and quality of the bow.

screw button    Parisian eye    frog    grip    winding    stick

back plate    slide    ferrule    bow hair

### Silver, gold, and nickel silver

Silver-mounted bows usually start at around five hundred dollars, and gold-mounted bows (rare, but they are around) may easily cost five times as much. Most cheaper bows have nickel silver mountings. Contrary to what you might expect, nickel silver does not contain silver.

### Full-lined

The frog in the picture above is a *full-lined frog*. A *half-lined frog*, usually found on cheaper bows, does not have the back plate behind the *slide* or extending underneath to the slide.

## CLOSE UP

Of course, there is more to a bow than the type of wood used and the mountings: the shape of the stick, for one thing, and the decorations on and around the frog.

**79**

### Eight-sided or round

The stick, which gets gradually thinner from the frog to the head, can be round or octagonal (eight-sided). Some cellists feel that octagonal sticks make for better bows, as they may be a little stiffer or more stable than round sticks.

### A little more

A bow with an octagonal stick, bow stick, or shaft usually costs a little more than one with a round stick — not necessarily because it's better, but simply because it takes more work to make one.

### Frog

On better bows, the frog is usually made of ebony, and sometimes of horn or (mammoth) ivory. Cheap bows often have plastic frogs. Most slides have a mother-of-pearl finish. The frog itself is often decorated with single or Parisian eyes. Intricately carved and decorated models are also available.

### Screw buttons

Screw buttons, also known as *end screws* or *adjusters* come in two- and three-part versions (i.e., silver-ebony, and silver-ebony-silver, respectively). Some have a single or a Parisian eye on each of the eight sides.

*Tensioning the bow hair: The frog moves backward.*

TIP

**Branded name**
Usually the name of the bow maker or the bow's brand is literally branded into the stick, just above the frog.

### Bow grip

The leather bow grip or *thumb grip* may be a little thinner on one stick than the next, and it may have tiny 'ventilation holes.' Instead of leather, vinyl is sometimes used on less expensive bows. This may feel a little sticky when you play. If the bow grip feels too thin, you can install a *thumb cushion*, which simply slides over it. If the grip is too thick, it's best to ask your violin maker or technician to replace it.

### Winding or lapping

Silver thread is usually used for the winding or *lapping*. Some bows have a silk winding or synthetic imitation baleen windings in one or two colors. The use of real baleen (whalebone) has been banned.

### Face

In the past, the protective *face* at the other end of the stick was often made of ivory. Today, bow makers use a synthetic material, metal, or bone.

## CHOOSING BOWS

When given the choice between a great instrument and a decent bow, or a decent instrument and a great bow, most professional cellists go for the latter combination. Some cellists even say your bow should cost as much as your cello. Others say half as much, or a quarter — so that's not much help.

Your best bow is the one you feel most comfortable with and the one that helps you to make your instrument sound its best, for a price you can afford.

### The best bow?

Which bow suits you best depends on both your bowing technique and on the style of music you play. A bow must suit your instrument too, and the strings you are using, so always try out bows with your own cello.

81

### More expensive

As with cellos, a more expensive bow is not always better, and an antique bow will often cost a lot more than an equally good new one (see Chapter 4). You can also get lucky and find a great bow for a bargain price. Even top cellists sometimes have a 'cheap' bow in their collection because it happens to be perfect for certain pieces of music.

### Suit the music

Again, the bow should suit the style of music you play. That's why cellists often have a variety of bows. Some bows are better for a bright, clear tone; others are preferable when the music requires a mellow timbre.

### Three by three

As with cellos, the best way to test a wide selection of bows isn't to try them all one after the other — you will probably have forgotten what the first one sounded and felt like by the time you reach the last one. Instead, concentrate on just two or three bows at a time. Compare them, reject the one you like least, pick out another, and so on. Play music that allows you to concentrate on the sound and the feel of the bow, rather than on the notes.

TIP

> ### Hair tension
>
> When comparing bows, take the hair tension into account.
> The 'best' tension may vary per bow, depending on the
> elasticity of the stick and your personal preference, among
> other things.

### Starting point

As a starting point, you may want to check the distance between the middle of the stick and the hair. If this is about 0.4" (1 cm), the tension will usually be about right — unless the stick has a deviant taper, for one thing.

### Different per bow

Turning the screw button the same number of times for each stick

82

isn't a good starting point, as this will probably result in very different hair tensions per bow. A tip: The number of times you need to turn the adjustment screw may vary on your own bow too, from time to time, depending on humidity and temperature. For example, low humidity will make the stick slightly stiffer, so the bow hair will be at the right tension sooner, and vice versa.

### What to play

Of course, the best test for any bow is to play the music you intend to use it for. Try out all the bowing styles you've mastered. Play slowly, fast, loudly, and softly, play *staccato* and *legato*, and keep listening and feeling how the bow performs and how it interacts with the instrument. Some bows respond better to the way you play and to where exactly you bow the strings than other models.

### Sound

A different bow will make you sound different, just like another instrument. In fact, there are even small differences between every two 'identical' bows. These nuances will often come out best if you play slow phrases, and you'll hear more of them when playing bows and instruments in the higher price ranges.

### Curved

A bow should be curved so that the hair, when slack, just touches the middle of the stick. If the stick is more curved than that, the hair may touch it when playing. Such a bow may also feel a little restless or jumpy. A bow that is too straight, on the other hand, may be sluggish. Looking on the bright side, you could also say

**Tipcode CELLO-007**
*This is what spiccato looks and sounds like.*

TIPCODE

83

*Setup with drum rack.*

that a more curved bow is good for *spiccato* (in which the bow bounces lightly off the strings), while a fairly straight bow would be better for slower phrases. But then, a really good bow should allow you to play anything…

### Flexibility

To check the flexibility of a bow, rest its face on a table and gently push it downward with your forefinger in the playing position. A very flexible bow can make it difficult to play fast pieces, but it may have a better tone than a stiffer model. Playing may be easier with a stiffer bow, but producing a good, long tone may become trickier. And again, a good bow should allow you to play anything you can. A tip: There are synthetic bows whose flexibility can be adjusted to match your technique or the music you play.

**TIPCODE**

**Tipcode CELLO-008**
*This Tipcode demonstrates how you can test a bow's flexibility. Always be careful not to damage the bow.*

### Weight

A full-sized bow usually weighs between 2.2 and 2.4 ounces (78–85 grams); usually, a bow weight of about 2.3 ounces is recommended. If you're looking for a full-bodied sound, you may want to find a relatively heavy bow.
Lighter bows are better suited for a lighter sound. If a bow is too light, it won't make the strings vibrate enough and you won't produce much sound at all.

### Small difference

Even the smallest weight differences can influence how you sound and play – and some cellists can spot the tiniest weight differences

**84**

between two bows. That said, differences in bow weights can be quite large, from less than 2.1 ounces (75 grams) for a baroque cello bow to some 2.9 ounces (102 grams).

### Balance
The heavier a bow is at the head end, the heavier it will feel. A top-heavy stick may be easier to guide. A stick with the weight further back feels lighter, but you have to guide it more. To compare bow balances, you can carefully balance them on your forefinger at about 9–9.5" from the end of the stick (not including the screw button). A bow's balance can be adapted by using more or less thread for the winding, for example, or even by making the tip heavier.

### Response
With some bows, the tone builds up very gently and gradually; with others the strings respond very quickly. To check the response of a bow, play lots of short notes on the lowest strings. Most cellists like to have a bow with an even response — in other words, a bow that produces the same response from the strings in the middle, near the head, and near the frog.

### In line
Look along the back of the bow, from the frog, to check that it is straight. Just like a cello neck, the bow must not look as though someone has tried to wrench it out of shape.

### Used bows
A few tips if you're planning to buy a used bow:

- If the hair is overstretched, a bow will feel very sluggish. The solution is to have the bow **rehaired** (see page 119).

- Another problem with overstretched bow hair is that the frog needs to be shifted very far back. This changes the **balance of the stick**.

- A bow can **lose some of its curve** or *camber* over the years. It may be possible to restore the curve, but be sure you know whether your bow is worth the expense.

- What Stradivarius is to the cello, **François Tourte** (France, 1747–1835) is to the bow. If you find his name on a bow, it probably won't be a real Tourte, unless it has a price tag of fifty thousand dollars or more.

### Brands

A few well-known bow brand names are Arcos Brasil, Ary-France, Dörfler, Höfner, Müller, Paesold, Seifert, Student Arpège, Roger, Werner, and W.R. Schuster. Low-cost synthetic bows are made by Glasser and P&H, amongst other companies; Berg, Coda, and Spiccato make more expensive and professional synthetic bows too.

### Workshop and master bows

There are also dozens of small bow workshops worldwide, especially in Germany and France, where bows of around three hundred dollars or more are made. Bows by independent makers, who work alone, start at around a thousand dollars, going up to ten thousand dollars and more. If a bow doesn't have a brand name at all, it's likely to be a very cheap one.

# ROSIN

Rosin makes the bow hair slightly sticky so it can properly 'grab' the strings and make them vibrate. When you play a string, the rosin makes it stick to the bow hair — until the tension gets too high as you move the bow along. At that point, the bow hair lets the string slip for a split second. This *stick-slip motion* is what makes the string vibrate.

### Many stories

Cellists often use the same type of rosin for years, but experimenting a bit can't hurt. A tip in advance: There are many stories about the differences and similarities of rosins, usually contradicting one another. Trying rosins out yourself is the best thing you can do.

_TIP_

## Hard

*Each rosin cake comes wrapped in a cloth or in a box so you're less likely to touch the rosin itself. Rosin is not only sticky, but also quite hard. As a rule, a cake will easily last you a year or longer, unless you drop it: Being as hard as it is, it may shatter into a zillion pieces.*

### Light and dark

Many companies sell rosins in two colors, at the same price: a light, honey-like color, and a darker color, almost like licorice. You often read that light rosins are harder and less sticky (so you should use these in the summer, when the higher temperature will make them softer). This may be true of some brands, but it can be the other way around just as well. Often, only the color is different. When you start playing, that difference vanishes as well: Rosin dust is always white.

*Rosin is sold in cloths and boxes, rectangular or round cakes, and in various colors.*

### Harder and softer

The rosin of one brand may be harder than that of another, and some brands sell rosin in different hardnesses. You may be able to feel the difference between the softer and harder types by pressing your fingernail into them.

### The best rosin?

Even experts don't agree on which rosin to choose. A few examples of their differing opinions? Softer rosin makes your strings respond better, but because it is stickier, it's more likely to produce

**87**

unwanted noise. You are less likely to get that type of noise if you use steel strings. On the other hand, rosin developed for steel strings is often harder than rosin designed for gut strings, supposedly because gut strings don't respond properly if you use a very hard rosin...

### Loud music, hard rosin?

Some experts, including both cellists and rosin makers, say that harder rosins are especially suitable for louder music, or when a fast response is required, or when the music you play requires a lot of bow pressure. However, other experts recommend harder types of rosin for quiet pieces; being less sticky, they would produce less noise.

### Sticky

An extra-sticky rosin tends to produce less dust, so less gets onto your cello. What's more, you won't need to apply as much pressure on your bow. On the other hand, this type of rosin is more likely to clog up your bow hair, which will then have to be cleaned more often. Some more expensive rosins, having finer particles, are said to produce more — and finer — dust.

### Barely noticeable

Many experts believe the biggest difference between the many types of rosin is the amount of dust they produce during application and just afterwards: Once you are playing, the differences are barely noticeable, if at all. Most experts agree that this is even more true if you use a student or intermediate bow.

### Confusing

Just to add to the confusion, the very same rosin is sometimes sold with a different package, label, price, and description. And while some manufacturers sell different rosins for cello, violin, and viola, others make just one for all three instruments. A couple of companies even make special types of rosin for electric cellos.

### Gold and silver

Rosins often cost between five and fifteen dollars, including varieties that contain gold or silver particles. The precious metal is said to add clarity and brightness to the sound — although not all cellists can tell the difference.

### New bow or strings

If you buy a new bow you may well need a different rosin to do it justice, and the same is true if you start using a different type of strings. Some manufacturers try to make it easier for you to match their various types of strings and rosins by producing rosins that bear the names of their strings. This can be useful, though it doesn't mean that it isn't worth experimenting with other brands and types too.

### Hours

Unfortunately, trying out rosins is a slow process: The old rosin will still be effective for several hours of playing after you've applied a new one. That's why cellists who use different rosins for different styles of music also have a different bow for each type of rosin — or a different type of rosin for each bow…

### Non-allergic rosin

If you're allergic to traditional rosin, try one of the hypo-allergenic or non-allergenic rosins available, or try a rosin that produces less dust. A hypo-allergenic rosin is less likely to cause a reaction, and non-allergenic rosins should not cause an allergic reaction at all.

89

# 8

# Accessories

*If you buy just a cello, rather than a complete outfit, you'll need to invest in a gig bag or a case. Other accessories for cellists are cello stands, mutes, and devices to suppress the stuttering sound of a wolf tone.*

Cello bags and cases are available in a wide variety of styles, the most expensive case easily costing twenty times as much as the cheapest bag. Bags are usually easier to carry around than cases; they weigh less and they're softer. Besides, most bags come with adjustable, padded backpack straps. On the other hand, a good case offers better protection against harder blows.

*Cello bag.*

### Cello bags

The cheapest cello bags are available for about forty dollars, but you may also find bags that cost four times as much. The price depends, among other things, on the padding (from none at all to an inch or more) and the quality of the bag itself. For example, 600 Denier nylon is denser and stronger than 420 Denier nylon.

**92**

## Pockets

Cello bags usually have pockets for your bow and strings, and possibly for other accessories or sheet music. A tip: Always take the bow out before unpacking the cello. This prevents damaging the bow. Another tip: To keep the inside of the bow pocket clean from rosin, put your bow in a separate, washable cotton liner bag.

## Cases

Most cello cases have a hard shell made of plywood, fiberglass or some type of plastic. To resist moisture, wooden shells are usually covered with vinyl, leather, or nylon or cordura cloth. Prices range from about three to eight hundred dollars and more. A good case will absorb a shock if it falls, and it's sturdy enough to resist being crushed if something heavy falls on it. The cheapest cases, their cores being less strong, may not offer enough protection.

*Fiberglass cello case.*

93

### Inside

A padded, plush-lined interior absorbs shocks and prevent scratches. The padding tends to be thicker in more expensive cases. If a choice between a velour or a velvet lining is offered, the latter will cost a little extra.

**TIP**

### Suspension cases

*In many cello cases, the instrument is suspended: The bottom is recessed at the back and the scroll of the instrument.*

### Protective cloth

Covering the instrument with a cloth before closing the case offers extra protection against damage and dirt from the bow(s). Some cases come with a cloth or a foam pad for that purpose.

### Bow holders

The inside of the lid usually has holders for two bows. A tip: Always put the bows in with their hair facing outwards. Separate bow cases for one or more bows are also available.

### Case covers

To prevent your instrument from getting wet when it rains, the case should close properly. For extra protection you may want to invest in a separate case cover. Covers are available with or without extra padding and sheet music pockets.

### Locks and hinges

Most cases are lockable. This is mainly to ensure that the catches cannot open by accident — for instance, if you drop your case — so make it a habit to always lock them. When choosing a case, check the locks, hinges, handles, and carrying straps carefully: Usually, these are the weak spots.

### Handles, wheels, and feet

Cases and bags often have two or even three handles, making it easier to take the instrument out of a car, for example. Some cases and bags come with (optional) wheels. It's advisable to use these on even, smooth floors only. To protect the case or bag from wear, it may have rubber or metal feet on the bottom and the sides.

> ### Hygrometer
> *Cellos are particularly sensitive to very dry air. Some of the more expensive cases available have a built-in hygrometer, so you can check humidity at any time (see page 131).*

**TIP**

### Cello stands
It's best to keep your instrument in its case or bag when you're not playing. For short breaks, however, it may be easier to place it on a cello stand, rather than lay the instrument on the floor or put it back in its case. Cello stands, available for around fifty dollars, usually have a holder for the bow too. A warning: The soft pads on

*A cello stand.*

95

some stands may leave imprints in the varnish, especially in high temperatures. Most cello stands are collapsible, so you can easily take them along. For home use, there are padded, box-shaped stands too.

### Two more tips

- If you don't use a stand and you need to lay your cello down for a minute, always put it **on its side** – never on its back or top.

- **Never lean your the cello up against the wall** or in a corner standing on its endpin. This is simply too risky.

# MUTES

If you place a *mute* on the bridge of your instrument, the sound becomes softer, mellower, or warmer: Mutes muffle some of the higher frequencies of the sound. If the composer wants you to use a mute, the score will show the instruction 'with mute' in Italian: *con sordino*. Practice mutes (see page 23) muffle the sound a lot more than regular mutes do.

### Bigger and heavier

As discussed on page 51, a heavy bridge may slightly muffle the sound of your instrument. A mute works the same way, basically: You make the bridge heavier by sliding a mute onto it. This extra mass absorbs a part of the vibrations of the bridge, so fewer vibrations are transferred to the body. The bigger or heavier a mute is, the more it will muffle the sound.

### Clothing pin

Want to try this out? Very carefully attach a wooden clothing pin to the bridge of your cello, and you'll hear that the sound will be muffled slightly. If you attach another clothing pin, doubling the added mass, the muffling effect will be even stronger.

### Variety

Mutes come in rubber, metal, or wood, and in a wide variety of

96

models. Most mutes are fairly inexpensive, costing between five and fifteen dollars.

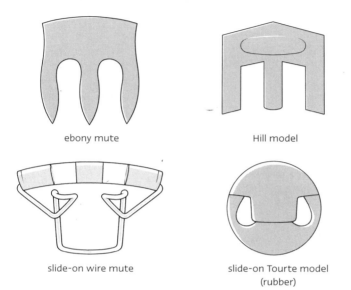

ebony mute                          Hill model

slide-on wire mute          slide-on Tourte model
                                   (rubber)

## Detachable or slide-on

The most basic mute, a three-pronged model, looks like a short, thick comb. You put it onto your cello bridge only when you need

*A slide-on wire mute at the tailpiece...*

97

it. Another type, the fixed mute or slide-on mute, stays attached to the instrument. If you don't need it, you slide it over the strings toward the tailpiece. Slide-on mutes come in rubber (e.g., the Tourte model) and wire versions.

*... and a rubber slide-on mute on the bridge.*

### Which one?

Slide-on mutes are especially easy in pieces where you have to change quickly between playing with and without a mute. There are some cellists who prefer never to use them because, even when they are near the tailpiece, they could muffle the sound (though you're unlikely to hear the difference), or because they might vibrate along with the strings. Others thoroughly dislike clip-on mutes, because they're easy to lose...

### A tiny bit

A wire mute can also be used to make your sound just a tiny bit sweeter. To do so, slide it to a position somewhere between the bridge and the tailpiece. The closer you get to the bridge, the stronger the muffling effect. You can also offset a wire mute diagonally, so that it muffles the high strings more than the low ones, or the other way around.

### Tone filter

To slightly mute one or more strings, you can also attach a rubber sleeve around them, at the bridge. An even faster solution is to use a small rubber disc, known as a *tone filter*, which can be put between the string and the bridge without removing the string.

> ### Take it off
> *Always remove the mute from your instrument before packing it up. If you don't, your cello could get damaged. Small mutes can stay put.*

**TIP**

## WOLF TONES

Many good cellos are plagued by *wolf tones*: At a certain pitch, the sound seems to stutter, or howl, like a wolf. If you want to check a cello for wolf tones or *wolfs*, play the notes D3 to F♯3 on both the G- and the C-strings. Occasionally, other pitches may produce wolf tones too. Try playing close to the bridge to bring out mild wolf tones.

### Spring-mounted weight

A wolf tone is the result of (a part of) the instrument vibrating at a speed that is very close to the note you play, as you will see below. A popular device used to fight wolf tones is basically a spring-mounted weight that compensates (and thus suppresses) these 'disturbing' vibrations. This device is to be installed inside the instrument.

### Other solutions

In some cases, the wolf can be eliminated by attaching a short metal tube to the relevant string between the bridge and the tailpiece. The best position is determined by trial and error. A mild wolf can possibly be suppressed by using a mute; by changing to a heavier or lighter bridge; by mounting a fractional-sized

**99**

tailpiece; by choosing lower-tension strings; or by replacing chromium-wound strings by tungsten- or silver-wound strings, for example. Putting a cork between the tailpiece and the top may work too, but this will also muffle the instrument's sound. Applying more pressure to the bow or clamping the cello with your knees as you play can prevent the wolf from becoming too active.

*A wolf tone eliminator.*

### How it works

If you want to know more about wolf tones, here's how it works — in very basic terms. At a particular note, (parts of) the instrument may start resonating very strongly at a frequency very close to the note you play. If you play E3, for instance, the string vibrates 165 times per second. If the instrument has a very strong resonance at,

## Fine instruments

*Ironically, cheap instruments are not very often plagued by wolf tones, simply because they don't have responses strong enough to cause them. Conversely, fine instruments hardly ever come without them.*

**100**

say, 160 vibrations per second, the wolf will stutter five times per second (165 minus 160).

## (Dis)appearing wolfs

Fighting a wolf is a matter of changing the relevant resonant frequencies of the instrument, which you do by adding weight. In some cases, the reverse may work as well. For example, violin makers have suppressed wolfs by shortening the fingerboard. As wolf tones may disappear by making changes to the instrument, certain repairs may also produce wolf tones. Replacing a bass bar is one of them.

# 9

# Tuning

*A cello has to be tuned before you can play it. When you start out, your teacher will help you tune your instrument, but sooner or later you'll have to learn to do it yourself. Is it difficult? No, but you'll only learn properly by doing it often. This chapter covers some basic techniques and tuning tips and tricks.*

On a well-adjusted cello, steel or synthetic strings don't easily go out of tune. Even so, you always need to check the tuning before you start playing.

### Steel strings and fine tuners

With steel strings, even the slightest rotation of a peg translates into a major difference in the tension on the string. That's why most steel-stringed cellos have fine tuners in the tailpiece (see page 55).

### Pretune

If you use steel strings, the tuning pegs are used only to roughly 'pretune' the strings. When doing so, make sure the fine tuners are in their middle settings, so you can use them to tune both up and down.

### Plucking or bowing?

You can sound the string you are tuning by plucking, as you would with a guitar. For beginners that may be easier, but you can hear what you're doing better if you bow the strings.

### The A

When you hear an orchestra or an ensemble tuning, their reference pitch is the A that you find to right of Middle C on a piano. This A is referred to as A4.

### An octave lower

The A-string of a cello sounds an octave lower: It is the A to the left of Middle C, also known as A3. All these notes are clearly shown on the piano keyboard on page 14.

### A piano at hand?

If you have a piano at hand, you can adjust the pitch of the A-string to this particular A on the piano.

### Tuning fork

Usually, however, there will be no piano around. In that case, you can buy a tuning fork — a thick, two-pronged metal fork. Tap it on your knee, gently put the stem against your ear or on the bridge of your instrument, and you'll hear the reference pitch A. This pitch can be played back on many electronic metronomes and electronic tuners too.

**Tipcode CELLO-009**

As you can see here, you can also tap a tuning fork on a table top and use the top as a sounboard to amplify the sound.

**TIPCODE**

Tuning fork in A=440.

## A4

Tuning forks sound the pitch A4, while your A-string is supposed to sound the pitch A3, an octave lower. This difference makes it a little more difficult to hear whether the A-string is tuned too high (*sharp*), too low (*flat*), or just right — especially if you're just starting out.

### The same pitch

Comparing your A-string to the reference pitch would become a lot easier if you could make the string sound an octave higher — and you can! You do so by playing the string while lightly touching it exactly midway, without pressing it against the fingerboard. If the string has been properly tuned, the *harmonic* you hear now sounds A4 exactly. Learning to play harmonics or *overtones* takes a little practice, but it's a very helpful technique for tuning.

**105**

**Tipcode CELLO-010**
*Lightly touching the A-string midway produces a harmonic that sounds A4.*

### Tuning the A-string

If the A on the cello sounds too low compared to your reference pitch, you'll have to raise the tension on the string by turning the fine tuner clockwise, and vice versa. If you can't hear whether the string sounds flat or sharp, try turning its fine tuner all the way down. Then you can be almost certain that it sounds flat. From there, slowly bring the pitch up.

### Singing

You can also sing along. First listen closely to the reference pitch and sing it. Then sing the pitch produced by the string. Usually, you will then 'feel' if you have to sing higher or lower, and you can adjust the string accordingly.

### In the middle

If you start with the fine tuners in their middle settings, you can typically tune each string up or down a whole step (whole tone) or even more. In most cases, this is enough to get them to the correct pitches.

### The D

Once the A is right, tune the D-string. On the piano keyboard on page 14 you can see that this D is five white keys to the left of A3. This tonal difference or *interval* is called a *perfect fifth*.

### Twinkle

If you don't have a piano at hand, you'll hear this interval when you sing the first two words of *Twinkle, Twinkle, Little Star*. To

tune your D-string to your A-string, you should sing the first
_Twinkle_ when playing the D, and the second, higher-sounding
_Twinkle_ when playing the A-string.

### Backwards
On the cello, all adjacent strings are a perfect fifth apart. As you
usually tune from high to low (starting with the A-string, then the
D, etc.), it may help to learn to sing _Twinkle, Twinkle_ backwards:
Sing the second _Twinkle_ while playing the higher-sounding string,
and match the lower-sounding string to the first, lower-sounding
_Twinkle_.

### Check
When you have tuned all four strings, check them once more.
Usually you'll have to adjust the tuning here or there. The nursery
rhyme will point you in the right direction. However, there is a
better way to check the tuning.

### Better still
The trick is to bow two adjacent strings. On a properly tuned cello,
these string pairs produce a pleasant, full sound. If they sound
slightly 'wavy,' the strings are not quite in tune, so carefully adjust
one of them. These 'waves' are known as _beats_. The slower these
beats get, the closer in pitch the strings are. As soon as the strings
are in tune with each other, the beats are gone.

### Press the string
If you still can't tell if a string sounds flat or sharp, try pressing

**107**

TIPCODE

**Tipcode CELLO-012**
*Here you can clearly hear the beats. If you hear four beats per second, the sounding pitches are four hertz apart.*

it very close to the nut. This raises its pitch very slightly. If this makes the pitch difference smaller (the beats become slower), you have to bring the string's pitch up a little. If it increases the pitch difference (the beats speed up), of course you need to slightly lower the string's pitch.

### Again: harmonics
Pitch differences (and the 'beats' they produce) between two strings become even clearer if you use harmonics again, as explained on page 105. First bow the A-string and lightly touch it exactly midway with your other hand; then bow the D-string and touch it at one-third of its length. You'll find that they both strings now sound a harmonic at the pitch A4. If not, you have to adjust one or both strings.

TIPCODE

**Tipcode CELLO-013**
*Comparing the harmonic midway the A-string to the harmonic at one-third of the D-string.*

### The other strings too
108
This trick works for the other adjacent string pairs too: Play the

harmonic at one-third of the lower-sounding string, and compare it to the one midway the adjacent higher-sounding string. You can easily play these two *touch harmonics* simultaneously, using your ring finger on one string and your thumb on the other, as shown below.

A4 on the
D-string

A4 on the
A-string

*Comparing string pitches with harmonics.*

---

### Too much noise

To be able to hear your strings' pitches even onstage while everybody else is tuning, simply press one of the tuning pegs of the bass strings to your ear. Works great.

---

### Left or right

Some cellists operate the fine tuners with their right hand, which may be awkward as you hold your bow in that hand too. Others prefer to do it with their left hand, which requires you to move your arm around the neck first. The advantage of left-handed fine tuning is that you can bow while you tune, which makes it easier to compare pitches. A tip: You may inadvertently press the fine tuners when operating them. If so, the pitch will drop as soon as you let go of them.

### Bowing

When you're tuning, try to make sure you bow with a consistent, light pressure. If you don't, the tuning may turn out to be less than perfect as soon as you start playing.

### With a piano

You can of course tune all your strings to the relevant keys of a (perfectly tuned!) piano, but you'll learn to tune better if you use the reference A only. After all, that's how you'll often have to do it if you play in an orchestra or in another group or ensemble.

### Press the pedal

If you do tune to a piano, always use the right (sustain) pedal. This will make the note sound for a long time, so the pitches of the piano and your cello are easier to compare.

### Pitch pipe

Pitch pipes are popular tuning aids. There are two types, those with one note (the A) and those with four (one for each string). Pitch pipes are cheap, but their pitches usually aren't very reliable.

### Chromatic tuner

An electronic *chromatic tuner* shows you exactly which pitch it is hearing, and whether it is flat or sharp. These devices, available for twenty-five dollars and up, are especially popular with guitarists. Cellists often say it's better to learn to tune by ear, because you also depend on your ears to hear whether you are playing in tune.

### Stretching strings

Strings stretch as they get older. Eventually they may come to a point where your fine tuners can't get them in tune anymore. If so, you'll have to tune them a little higher with your pegs. Before you do, first loosen the string with the fine tuner as far as it will go. *Tip:* If a string has been stretched this far, it probably needs to be replaced.

### Tuning with pegs

When using the pegs, it's easier to tune up than to tune down. So if a string sounds sharp, first turn the peg until the string sounds flat and then go back up from there, turning the peg backward in very small increments.

Apart from that, tuning with pegs is really the same as tuning with fine tuners, though it does take some time to learn how to adjust them. One tip: Pressing the peg in while tuning will help keep it from slipping.

**Tipcode CELLO-014**
*Tuning the cello with the tuning pegs.*

**TIPCODE**

### Seasons

Learning to tune with the pegs, even if you use steel strings, has the added benefit that it will help prevent the pegs from getting stuck when humidity is high (in the summer) or from suddenly slipping — and thus causing string damage — when the air is dry, in wintertime.

### A=440

The A (A4) that most orchestras and ensembles tune to vibrates 440 times per second. This pitch is usually referred to as A=440 hertz. A well-tuned cello A-string vibrates exactly half as fast (A=220).

**Tipcode CELLO-015**
You can tune you're A-string to this pitch (A=440).

## A=442

Some orchestras tune to an A that is a tiny bit higher. You can buy tuning forks for these tunings too, such as A=442.

**Tipcode CELLO-016**
The Tipcode demonstrates the slight difference between A=440 and A=442, as well as the resulting two beats per second when these pitches are played simultaneously.

### Scordatura

For some works, mostly modern compositions, cellos are required to be tuned differently. Such alternative tunings are known as *scordatura*. These tunings may make playing certain chords easier, for instance. Three examples are A, D, A, D; A, D, F♯ , B; and A, D, F, C (from high to low).

### Detune your strings?

A final tip: Do not release the tension of strings after playing, as this will hurt rather than protect your instrument and your strings. Do, however, always loosen your bow hair after playing.

# 10

# Cello Maintenance

Repairing and adjusting a cello are best left to an expert. But there is plenty you can do yourself to keep your instrument in the best possible condition: cleaning, replacing strings, straightening the bridge, finding buzzes, and much more.

The rosin from your bow settles on your cello as dust. You can easily wipe most of it off with a soft, lint-free cloth each time you finish playing. A cotton cloth will do fine — an old, unprinted T-shirt for instance, or a dishcloth. Be careful not to snag the edges of the instrument. On some finishes (e.g., synthetic finishes) you can also use a slightly damp cloth, if necessary. Don't forget to wipe the bow stick as well.

### Fingerboard and strings
It's best to use a different cloth for the neck, the fingerboard, and the strings where you touch them with your fingers. Wipe the strings with the cloth and then pull it between the fingerboard and the strings. Again, a cotton cloth is good for the job, but some cellists prefer to use silk. Once you've wiped your cello, put it back in its case or bag.

> ## Clean hands
> Strings will live longer if you wash your hands before playing, and your cello will be easier to keep clean if you hold it by the neck only.

### String instrument cleaners
Every cello needs extra attention once in a while, even if you are very careful. The top can get sticky and dull, especially between the *f*-holes, where most of the rosin dust ends up. You can remove this residue with a special string instrument cleaner. There are string instrument cleaners and cleaning cloths that polish your cello as well, smoothing away fine scratches.

### The best?
Which is the best cleaner for your cello may depend on its varnish, so always ask what you can and cannot use on an instrument when you buy or rent it. Before using a cleaner, always read the instructions. Then try a small area first, preferably one that's out of sight: Some delicate varnishes can be damaged by an abrasive polish, or by a cleaner that contains harsh solvents.

**114**

### Never

Whatever you do, never use ordinary household cleaners. One exception would be using a window cleaner on a synthetic or alloy tailpiece — as long as you spray the cleaner on a clean cloth first, rather than directly on the instrument.

### The fingerboard

You can occasionally give the fingerboard an extra cleaning by dabbing it with a soft cloth, moistened with a tiny bit of rubbing (or denatured) alcohol. To make absolutely sure that no liquid gets onto the varnish of the body, keep the bottle well out of the way and do not allow the cloth to drag over the body. For safety's sake, lay another, dry cloth over the body.

### The strings

To remove rosin residue, grime, and finger oils from your strings, you can push a clean cloth along them a few times, going from the top of the fingerboard to the bridge. Don't push too hard, and hold one hand across the strings, because they can really screech when you do this.

### Alcohol and steel wool

If this doesn't work, you may moisten the cloth with some rubbing alcohol, provided you don't use gut strings. Again, do not spill any of this liquid on the instrument. Special string cleaners are available as well. Some technicians remove rosin buildup with very fine steel wool. Always be sure to cover your instrument first before cleaning the strings!

### Inside

Over the years, dust and dirt will inevitably find their way into your cello. Some players clean inside their instruments by pouring a handful of dry, uncooked rice through the *f*-holes and gently shaking the body around a few times. Then they turn the instrument upside down and shake it some more. This cleans the underside of the top while pouring the rice as well as most of the dust out of the *f*-holes.

If you use this technique, though, there's always a risk that a grain will get caught inside (in a tiny gap between the lining and the

**115**

side, for example) and cause rattling, especially in instruments that are roughly made or have been frequently repaired.

### Splinters
When cleaning the instrument, make it a habit to check for splinters, especially around the edges, and other minor damage. The cleaning cloth or your clothes can pull these splinters off of the instrument, or the splinters can hurt you, or your clothes may get caught in them while playing...

### Expert
You need to take your cello to an expert when it needs more extensive cleaning, if there are stains that won't go away, if you can't get the neck clean, or if the varnish has become very dull (on the body, under the strings, or where you touch the body with your left hand). Many cellists have their instruments checked once a year, even if nothing seems to be wrong, just to be on the safe side.

TIP

### Plastic
*If your perspiration is especially acidic, it can damage the varnish and even the wood of the ribs where your left hand touches it. The solution? There are violin makers who stick a strip of self-adhesive plastic to the rib. Others makers are appalled at the very idea of sticking plastic to an instrument. As an alternative, you can try using a cloth or velvet bib.*

## TUNING PEGS AND FINE TUNERS

Fine tuners do not require much maintenance, if any at all. If one does get a little stiff, you may apply a tiny bit of acid-free Vaseline. Wooden tuning pegs, on the other hand, can be troublesome.

### Peg compound
The tuning pegs need to be able to turn smoothly, without

slipping back. This usually requires the periodic use of a little peg compound or peg dope. Other cellists prefer tailor's chalk, also known as French or Venetian chalk. If these treatments aren't effective anymore, you can clean the peg and peg hole with a little benzene. A stopgap solution for a slipping peg is to apply a bit of saliva to it. White chalk will help too, but it will also make the hole wear out faster. Some players use soap, but soap may congeal and make tuning harder.

### Loose

If a peg or the hole is badly worn, the peg can get really loose. Having a new set of bigger pegs custom-fit to the instrument will usually cost some hundred and fifty to two hundred dollars. This may or may not include the pegs, available from around seventy-five to a hundred dollars for a set. There are much more expensive pegs too, with golden rings or other decorations. If the peg holes are really worn out, they can be (re)bushed.

## THE BOW

Applying rosin is necessary only when the bow hair gets too smooth. That won't be more often than once or twice every week, even if you play a lot. The easiest test to see if your bow needs rosining is to draw a section of the hair over a dark cloth. If this leaves a white residue there's no need to apply new rosin.

**Tipcode CELLO-017**
This brief video shows you how to apply rosin.

**TIPCODE**

117

### Applying rosin

To apply rosin, draw the bow hair over the rosin rather than the other way around. You should cover the full length of the hair, from the tip to the frog. Keep your thumb on the ferrule to prevent it from damaging the rosin, and cradle the rosin so that you can extend several fingers above it to guide the bow.

### Rosin walls and fingers

Three more tips:

*   Prevent the bow hair from **wearing a groove in the rosin** (which will eventually leave 'walls' of unusable rosin) by rotating it now and again.

*   **Do not to touch the bow hair or the rosin** with your fingers, as finger oil and perspiration keep the rosin from holding onto the bow hair. If you need to touch the bow hair, e.g., to check the tension, do so with the back of your hand.

*   When using a brand new cake of rosin, some like to scratch its surface with a pin to '**get the rosin started**.'

### Excess rosin

After applying the rosin, wipe the bow hair with a cloth, or drag one of your nails across the bow hairs close to the frog. This ensures that the excess rosin doesn't land on your instrument. You can shake out your bow instead, but it's best not to: Even if you don't break anything or hit anybody, whipping the bow around in the air can damage it. A tip: If your sound becomes coarse or uneven after applying rosin, you used too much of it.

*The bow hair is held in place by small wooden wedges.*

wedge

face

### Grimy near the frog

If the bow hair gets grimy near the frog, you can clean it with a lukewarm, damp cloth, perhaps with a little liquid soap added to the water. If you do, be careful that the little wooden wedges that hold the hair in place are kept dry. If they get wet, they may expand and damage the stick.

### Cleaning the hair

If you need to apply rosin more and more often, that's probably due to old bow hair (have it replaced) or to a buildup of rosin residue, which makes the hair slick. Some cellists clean the hair themselves, using a cloth that's very lightly moistened with rubbing alcohol — but it is much safer to have it done by an expert. The liquid can easily damage the stick, and you may end up with the hairs sticking together, rendering the bow unplayable. A bow maker or technician can decide whether cleaning will help, or if rehairing is necessary.

### New hair

If the bow hair is overstretched, you'll never get the bow back to proper tension. The usual solution is a rehair. The same is true if too many of the hairs have broken. A rehair often costs some forty or fifty dollars. Sometimes, the bow hair can be shortened. Good-quality hair will last for years, and won't become wavy or brittle.

### Not tight

If you can't get the hair to the desired tension, the bow hair may be overstretched, or your bow stick could be slowly losing its curve. A bow maker or technician may be able to restore the curve.

### Broken bow hair

If a hair breaks, remove the loose ends by cutting them against the sharp edge of the ferrule or the face, rather than pulling them out. Another solution is to cut them carefully with scissors, as close as possible to the ferrule or face.

### Smooth frog

If the frog doesn't slide smoothly anymore, and the screw button feels stiff, cleaning them may help. Just turn the screw button

**119**

counter-clockwise until it comes off. Then you can remove the frog too. If the problem persists, it's best to have the bow looked at, which you should also do if the bow grip needs to be replaced, or if the frog wobbles.

### More tips
Two final tips:

- Be very careful **not to get your bow hair twisted** if you remove the screw and frog.

- Never use oil to lubricate the screw or the *underslide* (the part that lines the top of the frog), but gently **rub them with a candle**.

# REPLACING STRINGS

If strings break or if their windings come loose, you need to replace them. The same is true if your strings are getting older. Why? Simply because old strings get more and more difficult to tune, and their sound becomes duller and duller. The better your cello is, the better your playing, and the better your ear, the sooner you'll notice when strings need to be replaced.

### One string only?
If you replace a single string, you may find that it sounds a lot brighter than the older ones. If so, the only solution is to replace some or all of the other strings too. A tip: Used strings may still be useful as spares.

### Not more than two
If you want to replace your strings, never take off more than two of them at a time, so that the tension of the other two keeps the bridge and sound post in place. If, despite your precautions, the sound post does fall over, loosen all the strings and have the post set in position by an expert, who has a special tool for that purpose.

120

### The right order

In the pegbox, the two outer strings pass below the middle ones. This makes them harder to get to. So first remove one of the middle strings, and then the string that passes below it. Now replace the outer string, and then the middle one. An example: First remove the D-string, then the A-string; first replace the A, then the D; proceed similarly with the other two strings.

### Removing strings

To replace strings, sit down and lay the cello with its scroll on your left or right thigh, whichever is easiest for you. Take off the first string by slowly turning its tuning peg toward the body of the instrument, releasing the string's tension. If the peg doesn't want to move, pull it out slightly. Then pull gently on the string, so the peg will start turning until the string comes loose. Guide the string between your thumb and index finger near the pegbox, so that it can't suddenly come loose and cause damage.

*Most strings are attached to the tailpiece with a steel ball; gut strings often have a loop instead.*

**Tipcode CELLO-018**
*Removing a string (shown on a violin).*

**TIPCODE**

**121**

*Fitting a
new string.*

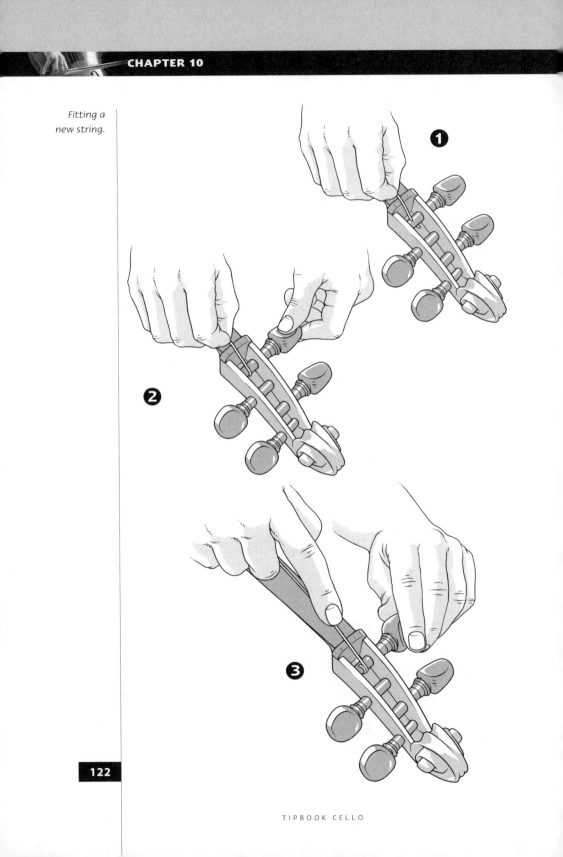

## Fitting strings

You can fit new strings in various ways. This is one simple way.

1. Turn the first peg so that the hole points diagonally upwards, facing the fingerboard.

2. Hook the ball end of the string in the fine tuner, or in the tailpiece slot. If the string has a loop end (gut strings) hook the loop in the tailpiece slot. Do not feed the string through its loop as if it were a lasso — unless the slot is worn out so it doesn't hold the string.

3. Stick the string through the peg hole (see illustration 1) and start winding it, turning the peg backward so the peg hole moves in the direction of the scroll.

4. Hold the string with your other hand so that it can't go slack and slip out of the peg, or come loose from the tailpiece (illustration 2).

5. Keep tightening the string, making sure that the windings run outwards, toward the thicker end of the peg. Use your index finger to keep the string tight and guide it through the groove in the nut (illustration 3). Also, make sure that the string doesn't wedge up against the inside of the pegbox.

6. Tune it so that it is at roughly the right tension, using the strings that are still in place for reference.

**Tipcode CELLO-019**
Fitting a string (again, shown on a violin).

**TIPCODE**

## Kink

If a string keeps on coming loose from the peg as you try to tighten it, take a pair of pliers and make a kink about half an inch (1–1.5 cm) from the very end of the string. The kink will make the string hook itself in place as you begin to turn the peg.

*Make a kink in each string. Lay the kink against the peg, and let the unwound part of the string wind around it a couple of times.*

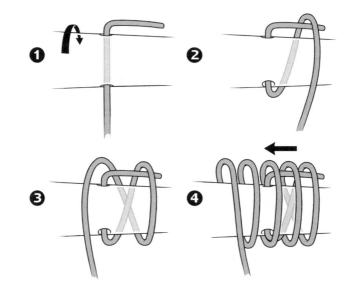

### Pegs in poor condition
Making a kink in the string can also help keeping your strings in place if your pegs are in poor condition. Stick the string through the peg's hole, and then lay the kinked end flat against the peg. Let the string run over it a couple of times as you turn the peg. Please note: Do not wind the plain (non-wound) part of a wound string around itself.

### Too long
If a string happens to be very long, you can first make sure it winds inwards for a few turns before guiding it back the other way. The last few turns must be wound directly onto the wood, and not on top of another part of the string. *Tip:* Four or five windings should be enough to prevent a string from slipping.

### Space
Strings can break if they are jammed against the cheeks of the pegbox. So always make sure they have some space.

124

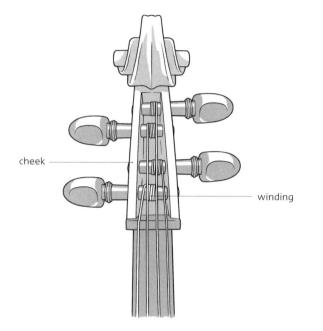

*Leave space between windings and cheeks.*

cheek

winding

### String sleeves

If you use string sleeves (see pages 75), slide them into place when the strings are nearly tuned.

### The first time

When you replace a string for the first time, you'll probably be short of hands. You need one to tighten the string; another to make sure it doesn't come loose from the tailpiece; a third to guide it through the grooves in the bridge and nut... So have someone else around to help.

### Grooves

When you replace your strings, check the pegs at the same time. Grooves in the pegs can damage your strings. If a peg won't 'grip' the string whatever you do, there's a chance that its hole is worn out.

TIP

**125**

### Sharp edges

Your strings can also be easily damaged by sharp edges on the bridge, the nut, or around the string holes in the pegs. The grooves in the nut must be smooth and nicely rounded to prevent the strings from kinking. Check your cello carefully if a string keeps breaking at the same point. If a string doesn't run smoothly across the nut or the bridge, twist the point of a soft lead pencil through the groove a few times. If that doesn't do the trick, you'll need expert help.

### Different strings

If you want to fit other types of strings than the ones you have used so far, there are some things to pay special attention to. First, if the new strings are thicker (for instance, if you replace steel strings with synthetic strings), the grooves in the nut and the bridge should be wide enough not to catch the strings and damage the windings.
Second, fitting higher-tension strings will raise the string height, and vice versa. This can be compensated for by adjusting or replacing the bridge, for instance.

### Perfect fifths

If you have a good ear, there's another way to find out it your strings need to be replaced. On a properly tuned cello, there is always a perfect fifth between one string and the next (see page 106).
You can check this by using a pencil to stop two adjacent strings in exactly the same position: Lay the pencil at a right angle across the two strings, and press them against the fingerboard. In both high and low positions, the difference in pitch between the two strings should always be a perfect fifth.

### Old strings

If you have old strings, this may not be so, perhaps because one string is more stretched than the other. If so, the first will sound flat. Old strings are not the only possible cause if you don't hear perfect fifths; the bridge may be the culprit instead. Another tip: If you use gut strings, you may not hear perfect fifths with this test either.

# THE BRIDGE

A cello bridge has to withstand a lot of force, the strings' tension both pulling it forward and pushing it into the body — so you do need to keep an eye on it.

### Perpendicular
Now and then, you should check that the bridge hasn't started leaning forward, toward the fingerboard. If it does, you can carefully try to push it back in its original position yourself, until its back is perpendicular to the instrument's top. Before doing so, first release the string tension a bit. A tip: Don't hesitate to leave this to a violin maker or technician.

### Perfect fifths
Another check: Make sure that both feet are lined up with the notches in the f-holes. If not, your instrument will not produce perfect fifths (see the previous page) and it will be hard to play in tune.

### New bridge
A bridge needs to be replaced if the downward pressure of the strings has forced it to bend, or if the grooves have got too deep: No more than a third of the diameter of each string should be inside the groove. A new type of string may require another bridge too. Another reason to have your bridge changed or replaced is that its top is too flat (so that you accidentally play two strings instead of one), or too curved (making it difficult to play two or three strings at once). A tip: Some violin makers may restore a bent bridge, which is cheaper than having it replaced.

*Bridge bending toward the fingerboard.*

**127**

### Summer and winter bridges

Dry winter air can make the wood of your cello shrink, in which case string height will be reduced. By the same token, higher humidity in the summer can make the wood expand, increasing string height. To compensate for these changes, you can use two bridges: a higher one for the winter, and a slightly lower summer bridge.

### Custom-fit

A new bridge needs to be custom-fit to the cello, so that it has the right height and curve for the instrument, and so that its feet match the top perfectly. Having a new bridge installed by a professional violin maker will often cost between seventy-five to hundred fifty dollars, the bridge itself costing less than the labor involved in installing it. A new bridge should last for years.

### More than carving alone

There are bridges with moveable feet that automatically adjust to the arch of the top. Even if you prefer this type of bridge, you should have a specialist install it: Again, properly fitting a bridge to an instrument involves more than carving the feet.

*A blank bridge (left) and one made to fit the instrument.*

# AND THE REST...

A cello is a fragile instrument that only gives its best if everything is in place, nothing that might produce a buzz is loose, and nothing is worn out.

**128**

### The sound post

If you have bought a new cello, it's a good idea to have it checked after six months or a year. One example of what an expert might spot is that the sound post may have become slightly too short as a result of the wood not having settled completely when you bought the instrument.

### The tailpiece loop

Another example would be that the tailpiece loop may have stretched. If so, the distance between tailpiece and bridge will now be too short, which may muffle the sound. On a full-size cello, the correct distance is about 4.5–5" (11.5–12.5 cm, i.e., ⅙ of the instrument's string length). To set this distance, tailpiece loops are often adjustable.

### The fingerboard

However hard your fingerboard is, stopping the strings will eventually wear grooves in it, and your fingertips will create shallow pits, especially if you perspire a lot. Of course, if you have a good, ebony fingerboard, this is a very slow process. Professional cellists, who play for many hours every day, often have their fingerboards reworked every one or two years. Replacing a fingerboard is expensive, because a lot of labor is involved.

---

**TIP**

### Splinter

*If a piece of wood breaks off — a splinter along the edge for instance — make sure that no moisture reaches that spot, and don't clean it. Take the instrument to a violin maker as soon as possible, and take the broken-off piece with you if you still have it. It's also best to see an expert if you find loose glue joints, or cracks. Do you feel like repairing these yourself? Don't!*

---

### Buzzes

A cello can start buzzing in all sorts of places. Some examples:

- If the bridge or the nut is **too low**, the strings may vibrate against the fingerboard.

- The **winding** of a string may be damaged.

- The **string ends** may vibrate if they are touching the pegbox or the tailpiece.

- While checking the tailpiece, have a look at the **fine tuners** too — especially the lock nuts.

- A **wire mute** or **loose purfling** can also cause unwanted noises, and so can an eye, or a decorative button on a tuning peg, or a loose glue joint.

*Purfling can come loose and cause buzzing.*

## *HUMIDITY*

Wooden instruments are very sensitive to dry air, and to rapid changes in humidity or temperature.

### *Freezing*

130

Dry air is especially likely to be a problem if it is freezing outside and the central heating is on full blast. If humidity gets too low, the wood of your instrument will shrink. The result? If you're lucky, you'll only find that the string height is reduced, and that you need a winter bridge (see page 128). If you're less lucky, the tuning pegs may suddenly come loose, which can result in string breakage, and it may get even worse: The top, the back, or any other parts can crack. The faster the humidity changes, the more dangerous it is.

### Hygrometers

The best level of humidity, both for cellos and for people, is often said to be around fifty to sixty percent. A hygrometer is a device that allows you to keep an eye on the humidity level. You may have one in the room where you keep your cello, and some cello cases have one built-in. If the hygrometer shows that the air is getting too dry or too moist, it's time to do something about it.

### Humidifiers

First, there are all kinds of small humidifiers that can be used inside the case, ranging from a very basic rubber tube with holes in it and a small sponge inside, to more complicated devices. Dampit is the best-known trade name. Prices are between about five and fifteen dollars, which sometimes includes a very basic humidity indicator. Cases with a built-in hygrometer often feature a humidifier as well.

### Sluggish

A dial-type hygrometer, which uses a hair to measure the humidity level, may become sluggish and less responsive after about a year. To solve this, leave it outside for a night, and the moist air will refresh it for a whole year. When the weather gets colder and you switch the heating back on, you can also wrap it in a wet cloth for a quarter of an hour and immediately afterwards set its pointer to 98%.

### All-around solutions

If humidity is very low in your house, then your instrument, your wooden furniture and floors, and yourself may benefit from a central humidifier (if your heating system allows for one) or a

131

portable one. Some examples of the latter are steam humidifiers (affordable, work fast, but may be noisy) and 'cold' humidifier systems, which are quieter but more expensive, take longer to work, and may need frequent maintenance (cleaning, filling, and so on). If humidity is very high, you may get a dehumidifier instead.

### Some time to adjust

Always give your instrument some time to adjust to changes in temperature and humidity. For example, if it's freezing cold outside and you enter a warm room, leave your instrument in its case for fifteen minutes, or as long as you can. The more gradually things change, the better your instrument will like it.

TIP

> **Heaters and vents**
>
> Some don'ts: Never store a cello in direct sunlight, or near heaters, fireplaces, air-conditioning vents, or anywhere else where it may get too hot, too cold, too dry, or too wet — not even if it's in its case.

# ON THE ROAD

A few tips for when you travel with your cello — which includes visiting you teacher:

- Make sure you have a **good case or bag**, and check now and again to make sure that the handles and carrying straps are properly secured.

- In the car, your cello is usually safest **on the back seat**.

- **Never leave your instrument in a car** for any length of time. Heat can rapidly build up and cause damage.

- Flying out? See if you can carry your instrument as **hand luggage**.

**132**

- If you do leave your cello behind somewhere, you're more likely to get it back if your **name, address, and phone number** are listed inside the case or bag.

- Just to be on the safe side: Always have a set of **spare strings** with you.

### Insurance

Consider insuring your instrument, especially if you're taking it on the road. Musical instruments fall under the 'valuables' insurance category. A regular homeowner insurance policy will not cover all possible damage, whether it occurs at home, on the road, in the studio, or onstage.

### Special insurances

Companies that offer special insurances for musical instruments can be found in string players' magazines or on the Internet (see pages 194–196). They may require you to have your instrument appraised before insuring it. Besides stating the value of the instrument, the appraisal report will also list various identifying features. You can list some of the essential data of your instrument yourself on pages 198–200.

### More tips

Two final tips:

- Most insurances do not cover **climatic damage**.

- Always check your insurance policy on the **conditions for air travel**.

# 11

# *History*

*Nobody really knows when the first cello was made,
and there are many, often contradictory stories about
its origins. In this chapter, you'll find some of the better
known highlights of the instrument's history. The details
can be found in many other books.*

In the days when dinner was still something you hunted, humans discovered that shooting an arrow produces a tone, due to the vibration of the bow's string.

### The eighth century

Only much later was it discovered that you can also make a string vibrate by bowing. Bowed instruments were probably being played in ancient Persia as early as the eighth century, and they were brought from Arabia to Spain not that much later. One of these instruments, referred to as either *rebab* or *rebec*, is often considered the ancestor of the violin family.

*Viola da gamba, a bowed instrument with frets and six strings.*

### Viols and violins

Eventually, two groups of instruments emerged from the rebab: the *violas da gamba* or *viols*, and the members of the violin family.

### Arms and legs

The violin family is closely related to the earlier *lira da braccio*. In fact, braccio instruments were played exactly like the violin — 'on the arm', as the Italian word *braccio* indicates. The violas da gamba, on the other hand, were played with the neck in an upright position. Their bodies rested on or in between the legs of the musician: *Gamba* is Italian for leg.

### Not the gamba

As you hold the cello between your legs too, people often think it stems from the viola da gamba. It doesn't, however: Violas da gamba are quite different. They have sloping shoulders and a flat back; they have C-shaped soundholes and more strings, which are tuned differently. They also have frets, like a guitar. These small ridges on the fingerboard make playing in tune easier.

### Violone

The cello was based on the violin, really. When Flemish composers started to use lower-sounding voices in their works, some time in the fifteenth century, musicians needed lower-sounding instruments than the violins and violas of that time. Consequently, various larger versions of the violin were built. These instruments were initially known as *bass violins* or *violones*. Violone is Italian for 'large violin.'

### Small large violin

The instrument that eventually became the cello was not the largest of these instruments — so the Italians called it *violoncello*, which literally means 'small large violin…' Only much later, around 1765, was the term violoncello abbreviated to cello or 'cello.

When talking about the very first cellos, people often refer to the instrument shown on a fresco from 1535 by the Italian painter Ferrari.

137

### Andrea Amati

Andrea Amati is usually considered the first maker of cellos, and some of his instruments are still around. Amati's cellos were of a quite large design, with a body of about 31.5" (80 cm). These larger instruments are often referred to as *church basses*.

### Antonius Stradivarius

The development of the slightly smaller, modern cello started in the late seventeenth century. Musicians wanted a smaller instrument because it would be easier to play: The string tension would be lowered and the distance between the positions on the fingerboard reduced.

Around 1707, Stradivarius, still the world's most famous violin maker, started to make these smaller cellos. Eventually, he created the standard model that's still being used by makers today.

### Violins versus viols

It took the cello a long time to replace the viola da gamba. For many years, the members of the violin family were looked down upon by the upper class. They were used for dance music, at parties, and in parades, while 'serious' music was played on the more delicate and softer-sounding violas da gamba. Incidentally, the viola da gamba is still being used today to play the music of that era.

### Solo

For many years, the cellist's role was solely to accompany other instruments — one of the reasons why it has been called bass or bass violin for so long. Antonio Vivaldi (1678–1741) was one of the first composers to write cello solo concertos. The first compositions for unaccompanied cello date back to the late seventeenth century. The violin was used as a solo instrument long before the cello.

### End pin

The end pin was probably introduced in the 1840s by the Belgian cellist Adrian Servais. Until then, the instrument usually rested on the player's calves.

### The bow

The very first bows had an outward curve, like the type of bow you shoot arrows with. Slowly the design changed to an inward curved stick. Around 1790, François Tourte (see page 86) designed the standard for today's bow.

### From gut to synthetic

Wound strings were already in use in the mid-seventeenth century. Steel strings became popular in the 1920s, followed by synthetic-core strings in the 1950s.

# 12

# The Family

The violin and the viola are the cello's closest relatives,
followed by the double bass. Most other bowed
instruments are either traditional or ethnic instruments,
from the rabab to the kemenche and the Hardanger fele.
The youngest relative, the electric cello, is covered at the
end of this chapter.

As was explained in the previous chapter, the cello is a descendant of the violin. It's not just a bigger violin, though. If you applied the violin's dimensions to the cello, its body would have to be about 40" long (much longer than it is), and it would only be some 3.5" deep. Such instruments, usually referred to as tenor violins, have been built but they were never successful.

**TIPCODE**

**Tipcode CELLO-020**
*The violin can be played in a wide variety of musical styles.*

### The viola

The viola is just a bit larger than the violin. It's tone is slightly lower, and also a bit darker and fuller. A viola is tuned to the same notes as a cello, but an octave higher: The A-string sounds the same pitch as the reference pitch most musicians tune to (A4).

### The double bass

The double bass, the lowest-sounding bowed instrument, looks like a mixture of the violin family and the viola da gamba. For

**TIPCODE**

**Tipcode CELLO-021**
*This is what the double bass sounds like, both plucked and bowed.*

Violin

Double bass

example, it has the *f*-shaped toneholes and the fretless fingerboard of the violin and the cello, but its (usually) sloping shoulders stem from the viol family. A bass is tuned differently as well, the strings being a fourth apart, rather than a fifth. They're tuned to E, A, D, G, from low to high, just like a bass guitar. The double bass is often used outside classical music, in which case it is usually plucked instead of bowed — again, like a bass guitar.

# ETHNIC AND TRADITIONAL INSTRUMENTS

Most of the other members of the bowed string family are quite rare, and you'll usually find them only in the hands of ethnic musicians or musicians who play older styles of music.

### Bourdon strings

The *viola d'amore*, for instance, is one of the bowed instruments that has a set of regular strings as well as some *bourdon strings*. These strings are not bowed or plucked, but they vibrate sympathetically with everything you play. The lira da braccio (see page 137) had bourdon strings or *off-board drones* as well.

### Fele and rabab

There are many other bowed instruments with bourdon strings. The Norwegian *Hardanger fele* is a smaller type of violin that has

*An Afghan rabab with twelve bourdon strings.*

four of them, and there are no less than twelve bourdon strings on the Afghan *rabab* shown below.

### Many names, many shapes

As discussed in the previous chapter, the predecessor of the violin was also called rebab. Today, this name is used for a wide variety of bowed instruments, some with and some without bourdon strings.

### Kemenche, kamaché, kemângeh

The same goes for the *kemenche*. This name may refer to a small, pear-shaped instrument with three strings used in Turkish classical music. But it can also indicate an elongated three-stringed instrument used to play folk music around the Black Sea and in Greece. The spelling varies as much as the shape, from *kemânje* to *kamaché* and *kemângeh*, and similar instruments are sometimes referred to as rebabs (or *rababs*, *râbabs*, and other spellings) as well. They're mostly played with their tail on the knee of the musician, with the neck held upright, like a viola da gamba. Incidentally, you may even see musicians who play a regular violin that way. And today's *rebecs*? They come with two, three, or more strings, with various body shapes, with or without frets…

*A kemenche.*

### With a fingernail

On some of these instruments, the different pitches are made not by stopping the strings on the fingerboard, but by touching them very lightly with a fingernail. The bow stick is often straight, and

**145**

you tension the bow hair not with a frog but simply by putting your fingers or thumb between the stick and the hair.

### Many more
Many other cultures have their own bowed instruments too, from one-stringed Indian to tubular Native American models. The format of this book doesn't allow listing them all, but there are other books that do.

# CELLO VARIATIONS

Many variations on the cello have been designed over the ages. Most of them disappeared within a decade or so after they were introduced; others lasted a little longer, but none survived as long as the current members of the family.

### Piccolo and tenor
In between the cello and the viola, for example, was the four- or five-stringed *violoncello piccolo*. *Violoncello tenor* is one of the names used for instruments that sound an octave lower than the violin — just as the cello sounds an octave lower than the viola.

### Portable cellos
Other cello variations were developed to improve the instrument's portability. One design, the *violoncello portatile*, had a detachable

TIP

### More variations
Making variations on the cello is not a thing of the past. Today's models are usually one-of-a-kind, custom-built instruments. One of the numerous examples is a five-string cello (D, A, D, A, D) with ten bourdon strings, designed to play Indian music. Another fine example is a 12-string cello (E, A, D, G, C and seven sympathetic strings below) with a pickup.

146

neck that could be stored inside the rectangular body of the instrument. The *porta cello*, built around the middle of the twentieth century, featured a smaller, though traditionally curved body and retractable knee rests.

### A new violin family

The Violin Octet is a group of eight violins of a new type, ranging from a seven-foot contrabass to a treble violin that sounds an octave higher than the traditional violin. The instruments have an increased resonance, volume and frequency range, allowing them to be used in electronic music and large venues, for example.

# ELECTRIC CELLOS

If you play your cello in a band, you're likely to find that it isn't loud enough. This can be solved by using a regular (vocal) microphone, but you can also add a special pickup to your instrument, or you can buy an electric cello specifically designed for playing amplified music.

### Electric/acoustic

You can amplify your instrument by supplying it with one or two *pickups* or *transducers*. These small, flat 'sensors' are usually wedged between the wings of your bridge. They literally pick up the vibrations of the strings and convert them to electric signals that can be amplified. As this solution allows you to play your instrument unamplified (acoustically) too, you could consider the result an *electric/ acoustic cello*.

### Clip-on microphone

Some types of transducers (i.e., *piezo pickups*) can make your instrument sound less warm and natural than a microphone would. That's why some cellists prefer to use a miniature clip-on microphone. However, using a microphone can easily cause feedback (the loud skreee you hear when someone points a microphone at a loudspeaker), especially if you need to play really

147

*Electric cello
(Zeta).*

loud. A best-of-both-worlds
solution is to use a pickup as
well as a vocal microphone on a
stand, or a dedicated system that
combines a pickup and a clip-on
microphone, with a control to set
the balance between the two.

### Electric cellos

If you plan to play electric only,
you can consider buying an
electric cello. These instruments
have no soundbox, but a small,
often solid body instead. Played
without an amp, you hardly hear
a thing. This makes them ideal for
silent practicing sessions. Some
electric cellos were specifically
designed for that purpose (see
pages 24 and 25).

### Chest and knee rests

To be able to hold the small-
bodied instrument just like
a regular cello, most electric
models come with chest and
knee rests. Usually they're
detachable for easier
transportation and storage.

### Shapes, designs, and prices

Electric cellos come in a wide
variety of shapes and designs,
often with more than four
strings, and with tuning
machines rather than the
traditional wooden pegs. Some
brand names in this field are

148

> ## MIDI
>
> *Some electric cellos can be hooked up to synthesizers, effects devices, computers, and other digital equipment, using a system called MIDI (Musical Instrument Digital Interface).*

TIP

Jensen Instruments, New Epoch, NS Design, Starfish Designs, Strauss, T.F. Barret, Violectra, and Zeta. Prices range from a thousand to seven thousand dollars and up.

# 13

# How They're Made

*Good cellos are still made in much the same way as they were hundreds of years ago, with chisels and files, with saws and planes, and with glue. Making a cello top in the traditional way easily takes a master violin maker several days' work.*

In a string instrument factory, machines are used for parts of the process, such as roughly shaping all the wooden components. Master violin makers who build an instrument by themselves from start to finish, still do everything by hand. Somewhere in between these two extremes are the workshops that buy unvarnished *cellos in the white*, which are finished by hand and provided with fittings and strings.

### Cake

The top and back are usually made of *quarter-sawn* or *quartered wood* — wood that has been sawed from the tree trunk in the shape of slices of cake. Each slice is then sawed almost in half to enhance the drying and seasoning process of the wood, which will make it less likely to warp, split, or shrink later on.

*Quarter-sawn wood is stronger that slab-cut wood.*

### Bookmatched

This slice is later sawed through completely to make two halves. These are folded open, like a book, and then glued with their backs together. The result is the beginning of a *bookmatched plate*, the two halves being each other's mirror images. Not all plates are bookmatched.

### Carved

Traditionally, the top and the back are then carved into shape. Using dyes and thickness gauges (graduation calipers), and simply by feel, the violin maker keeps checking to see if any more wood needs to be removed.

### Ribs, blocks, and lining

The ribs of the instrument are either moistened or heated so they can be shaped, then glued to the top, bottom, and corner blocks that strengthen them at the joints. The rib structure is assembled around a wooden mold. Small strips of woods (the lining) where plates and ribs meet are necessary to properly glue these parts together.

*Folded open like a book, then glued together.*

### Cut by hand

The *f*-holes and the channel for the purfling are traditionally cut by hand. Making the bass bar also takes a long time, as it has to be made to fit the inside arch of the top exactly.

corner blocks — top block

bottom or end-pin block

*... assembled around a mold...*

### Jigsaw puzzle

The neck and scroll are carved from a single block of wood. The neck slots into the top block like a piece in a jigsaw puzzle. The weight of the fingerboard, which is made of heavy ebony, is reduced by hollowing out the underside.

153

### Mirror-smooth

Before it can be varnished, the wood has to be made mirror-smooth with a scraper. It is finished with a base coat and several coats of varnish. Violin makers often make their own varnish, so they can give their instruments exactly the color and characteristics they are looking for.

### Bows

The bow stick is cut by hand, and its camber is shaped over a flame. The horsehair is held in place in the frog and head by small wooden wedges.

### Wonderful stories

There are lots of wonderful stories told about secret methods used by makers of those expensive old Italian cellos. For instance, it is said that the wood used to make them was transported by dragging it behind a sailing ship, and that it is the salt seawater that gives the instruments their special sound. Others say that the wood comes from centuries-old church towers that burned down; the wood was first broken in by vibrations from the church bells and then ripened by the fire... A more recent theory claims that Italian winters used to last longer and summers used to be colder, making trees grow slower and produce a higher quality wood. The coldest era lasted from about 1645 to 1715, and Stradivarius built his best instruments between 1720 and 1720.

154

# 14

# Brands and Makers

When you go out to buy a cello, you'll come across
dozens of brand names — names of violin makers young,
old, or dead, names of violin makers who never even
lived, brand names and names of countries, towns,
and regions. This chapter sheds some light on the cello
market, and it introduces you to some of the famous old
masters.

When you go shopping for a cello, you're bound to come across dozens of German names: Germany has always had a great reputation for producing good instruments in every price range. As a result, many cellos bear a German name, even though they have been made elsewhere, either in Europe or in Asia. Chinese bowed instruments are very popular, and Italy has a rich heritage when it comes to bowed instruments.

### Brand names

A certain brand name may be given to cellos made by various different workshops or factories — or a single brand name may be used for cellos with components from three different countries, which are assembled in a fourth country, varnished in a fifth, and shop-adjusted by the distributor or dealer. In other words: the brand name on a cello doesn't always tell you much about the instrument's origins.

### Quality

On the other hand, of course, there are many companies whose (brand) names can be seen as a guarantee for a certain quality. Some examples would be **Becker**, **Otto Brückner**, **F. Cervini**, **Glaesel**, **Knilling**, **Meisel**, **Palatino**, **Pegasus**, **Scherl & Roth**, and **Wm. Lewis & Son**, and other names mentioned in this chapter. Please note that these lists are not intended to be complete, and that brand names can be discontinued, sold, or changed.

### Germany

The German towns of Bubenreuth, Mittenwald, Klingenthal, and Markneukirchen are famous for their violin-making traditions and for the instruments made there today. A few of the better-known names are **Götz**, **Höfner**, **Paesold**, and **Stein**.

### Eastern Europe

Many of the founders of German string instrument companies came from the Czech city of Luby, which is often referred to as the 'Czech Mittenwald.' Other Eastern European countries, such as Hungary, Romania, and Bulgaria also have long cello-making traditions, from master instruments to low-priced, factory-made student cellos. Some brand names include **Dvorak**, **Lidl**, and

**Strunal** (Czech Republic), **Grygo Petrof** (Bulgaria), and Bucharest and **Vasile Gliga** (Romania). The Romanian center of violin making is Reghin.

### China
Most student and intermediate cellos and violins, with prices up to a thousand or two thousand dollars – and more – come from China, offering great value for their price. Three of the many, many Chinese bowed instrument makers are Ren Wei Shi, Samuel Shen, and Xue Chang Sun.

### France
France no longer produces large numbers of cellos, but two hundred years ago the French town of Mirecourt was home to the world's first string instrument factory, employing some six hundred people. The prices of old French factory-made instruments are usually a little higher than those of comparable German cellos. The French ones sound a little louder and brighter than the German models, some cellists say. Others claim to hear the opposite.

### Other countries
In most countries you'll be able to find master violin makers who create high-quality instruments entirely by hand, usually to order. Most of them also sell older instruments in various price ranges, bows, and accessories, and they repair, rebuild and sometimes rent instruments too.

### (Master) violin makers
Not everybody who uses the name 'violin maker' is a master violin maker. Some mainly do repairs of student and intermediate cellos, or they specialize in expensive instruments only; others concentrate on finishing and setting up white cellos (see page 152), and so on.
The exact number of master violin makers is unknown, but there must be over a hundred of them in the US alone. Most countries have an association or federation of violin and bow makers, which you'll be able to trace on the Internet or in string players' magazines (see pages 194–196).

157

# OLD MASTERS

Many books list the stories of dozens or even hundreds of violin makers from the past, where and when they lived and worked, and what their instruments could be worth today. Still, there's a good chance that the maker of your old cello won't be mentioned, simply because there are too many of them. Here's a very short introduction to some of the most famous names.

### Italy

The most famous Italian cellos were built in the town of Cremona, from the sixteenth century onwards. **Andrea Amati**, who presumably died in 1577, was one of the first violin makers. His grandson **Nicolo Amati** taught the craft to **Francesco Ruggieri** (also spelled as Ruggeri; 1620– c.1695), the most famous member of another important Cremonese violin-making family. Another of Nicolo's pupils was **Antonio Stradivari** (often referred to as Stradivarius), who lived from 1644 to 1737. Stradivarius also made harps and guitars. Of his bowed instruments, around six hundred have survived. **Domenico Montagnana** (c.1680–1750) and **Joseph Guarnerius del Gesu** (1698– 1744), the best-known member of the Guarnerius family, were among Stradivarius' students.

### Outside Cremona

Apart from the Cremonese school, to which all of these violin makers belonged, there were also other schools. Each had its own characteristics, such as the shape of the *f*-holes, or the precise model of the body or the scroll. The double purfling was one of the characteristics of the Brescian school. This school was founded by **Gasparo di Bertolotti**, known more commonly as **Gasparo da Salò**.

### Germany

Jacob Stainer, who died in 1683, is often seen as the founder of German violin making. Until well into the eighteenth century, an instrument made by Stainer was more expensive than a Stradivarius; the latter was often considered 'too loud.' **Mathias Klotz I** (1656–1743), who was very important for violin making in

158

Mittenwald, studied under Stainer and Nicolo Amati. Instruments made by his sons Sebastian and Georg are still highly prized.

### Other countries

Two important French makers were **Nicolas Lupot** (1758– 1824) and, from Mirecourt, **Jean Baptiste Vuillaume** (1798–1875). One of the best-known English names is **Hill**, a company where various violin makers and bow makers worked. You often find the description 'Hill model' on tailpieces, tuning pegs, mutes, and other parts. **Hendrik Jacobs** (1630–1704) and **Johannes Cuypers** (1724–1808) were two of the main Dutch makers. Some of the early American makers were **August Gemünder**, **Abraham Prescott**, and **Benjamin Crehore**.

# 15

# Tips on Practicing

*Practicing doesn't seem to be every musician's favorite pastime, and that goes for musicians at all levels and ages. Why? Because most musicians want to play their favorite music, rather than spending hours playing scales, etudes, or arpeggios. Because, oftentimes, progress doesn't show right away. And because learning to play an instrument is about long-term gratification, and we seem to have lost touch with that concept. Or because... A number of reasons. But still, it needs to be done -- and it can be entertaining, too!*

This chapter offers helpful hints on how to practice efficiently, turning practice sessions into rewarding and even inspiring events. Ineffective practice habits are as much work as effective ones, but yield no progress and may cause you to quit playing entirely. Also included in this chapter are helpful tips on where and when to practice, the various components of a good practice session and how to structure it, practice techniques, the importance of memorizing music, and much more.

### Sports

Practicing is to music what training is to sports, but there are some major differences. Firstly, most sportsmen train with their teammates, while practicing is something you usually do alone. Secondly, if you play football, soccer, or any other type of sport, you'll probably have a match every week. Most musicians don't have that many opportunities to perform — and usually, being able to perform is why you practice in the first place.

### Joining a band

That's why it's important to play in a band, an ensemble, or an orchestra: This offers performance opportunities, it's a great way to meet new friends, and it provides you with clear and realistic goals. Practicing so you can play your part at the next rehearsal is a better motivation than practicing because, well, you're supposed to.

### One note

Joining an ensemble is even more important if your play violin, cello, flute, saxophone, or any of the other instruments that typically produce one note at the time. These instruments are best suited for group settings, or should at least be accompanied by a piano, for example. Some other instruments that you'd rather play in a group are drums and the bass guitar.

### Just by yourself

The piano, keyboards, and guitars are better suited to playing just by yourself, without a band or another form of accompaniment — but even then, playing with other musicians is both fun and inspiring.

### Keep on going

It's clear that practice is necessary to achieve a certain level. But should you continue to practice once you've reached a level you're happy with?

Maybe not — but if this means that you're limited to playing the same pieces over and over, boredom may set in and the end of your musical endeavors may be near.

### No practicing

So can you play without practicing? Of course you can. There are thousands of garage band musicians who never practice; they just play with their friends, and they're having a ball doing so. However, they will usually stop playing once they get a little older, and having no real musical basis, it's unlikely that they'll pick up an instrument again later on in life.

### Recreational music making

Participating in a drum circle, for example, allows anyone to play music with a group of people without any prior experience. These and other recreational music-making activities are about socializing, reducing stress, and relaxation more than striving for musical prowess. (Incidentally, that's what most garage bands are about, too.)

### Not another obligation

If you want to pursue a career in music, your practice habits should foster diligence, hard work, and making sacrifices (though the latter may not be considered as such). If you don't, practicing should probably be more about fun than about obligations.

### Means, goal, or making music?

Some tend to see practice as a goal in and of itself; and the goal is achieved by practicing, say, a half an hour a day. Others consider practice a means to an end — the end usually being the ability to play well (at whatever level) and to perform successfully. You can also consider practice as making music, as a journey that leads to who knows where, and the journey itself is what it's all about. Teachers who make you understand and feel that playing scales is essential will help you enjoy this journey.

**163**

### How long — or how?

One of the most frequently asked questions is, 'How long should I practice?' You could certainly structure your practice sessions to last a required number of minutes per day. But wouldn't it be more interesting to look at what should or could be achieved, so your focus would be on accomplishing a particular task, rather than on filling time? Still, no matter how you look at it, you do need to invest some time in practice, and it's essential to be able to gauge how much time that typically is, so that's what the next section addresses.

### The youngest musicians

For very young musicians, things are a bit different. Most experts seem to agree that you can't really speak of 'practicing' until kids are some five or six years of age. For these kids, it's more about spending quality time and having fun with their instrument (if they've actually already chosen one) than about trying to achieve something other than a long-lasting love for music. Playing up to five or ten minutes a day will be fine.

The shorter these 'practice' sessions last and the more fun they are, the more likely a child will want to play three, four, or more days per week.

### Six and up

As children get a little older, they'll be able to focus for longer periods, and they'll start to grasp the concept of doing things now that will pay off later. They will also be ready to maintain a practice routine with their teacher's and your guidance. Six- to eight-year-olds should typically spend some fifteen minutes per day on an instrument, say four to six days per week. The older they get, the longer they will be able, and willing, to play.

### Half an hour

If you're older — twelve and up — most teachers will probably tell you that playing half an hour a day will help you make sufficient progress to keep things interesting. If you practice effectively, however, you may be able to do your assignments in less time. (This can be so rewarding that you end up playing longer than you intended!)

164

### Short and often

For kids, a practice session lasting a half an hour can be quite long, though, and it may be better to divide the routine up into three ten-minute sessions, or even six sessions of five minutes each. You can do so yourself, too: Short sessions tend to be more effective, with improved retention and more focus.

TIP

### Much longer

*The better you get, the more you need to practice to progress and maintain your abilities at a desired level. Music majors often practice three to five hours a day. The longer you practice, the sooner you will find that not practicing decreases your musical abilities — so you have to keep up all, or most, of the time!*

### Music, not minutes

Rather than focusing on a certain amount of time you need to practice, you can look at what should or could be achieved by practicing so you can focus on a set goal (and the music) rather than at the minutes passing by. In order to do so, you must understand exactly what your teacher expects (or you need to be able to set your own goals), and you need to be able to self-assess whether you've achieved those goals.

For teachers, this means that they need to be very explicit about their assignments. For example, rather than simply telling you to "learn to play that piece," they must state specific criteria, (i.e., "play it with the metronome at 148 beats per minute," or "play a scale five times, without any mistakes, at a certain minimum tempo"). This way, you can simply tell when you've completed the assignment.

If the teacher also conveys the practice techniques you need to most effectively reach the goals set for that week, practicing will be much more than a thirty-minute routine to be endured. It also puts things into your own hands, rather than in the clock's hands...

**165**

### Your own teacher

Practicing is something that needs to be learned (and often taught). When you practice alone, you're expected to catch your own mistakes, to discover what prompted them, to fix them, and to find a way to prevent them in the future. In effect, when you practice, you are your own teacher. That's not an easy thing to be.

### At home

And after all that, when you get to your next lesson or performance, you may find that you're not able to play what you could play at home. Or could you? Did you really hear everything that went wrong? Did you repeat everything to a point where you could even play it under pressure? Probably not — and playing in front of a teacher, your family, or any other type of audience is quite different from playing when there's no one around. This can be practiced too, though. Simply ask your roommate, your kids, friends, or anyone else to come listen to the new piece you have — hopefully — mastered. Getting experienced in playing for others is an important part of the learning process.

### When

Ideally, practicing becomes a daily routine, something which is as natural as having dinner, or brushing your teeth. And just like most people have dinner or brush their teeth around the same time every day, practicing is more likely to become a natural part of the day when you do it at or around a set time. Spending time with your instrument on a regular basis may be more important than how much practice you actually do, initially.

### Every day?

Should you practice every day? It's unlikely that anything you *have* to do seven days a week will be a lot of fun. That's why many experts will advise you that practicing five to six days will do to make sufficient progress.

### Which day?

The Sunday often sounds like a good day to skip practicing — but it's also the day of the week that allows for more time to practice, and practicing on Sundays still leaves plenty of time for other activities.

**166**

**A *closer* look**

*If you're having lessons, the day before your lesson is usually the worst one to skip. Also note that it's often very effective to have a short practice session right after your lesson or later that same day. This reinforces the lesson content, and it's a perfect opportunity to take a close look at your weekly assignments.*

### No time

If it's simply to busy for your intended practice routine, try to sit down and just play one of your favorite pieces, or something else you like to play, rather than not playing at all. Keeping in touch with your instrument is really important.

### When?

For many people, it seems best to practice at a set time or moment of the day (before school, right after work, before or after dinner…). Others prefer to schedule their practice time around other obligations. That way, they can play when they feel like it, rather than having to do so because it happens to be 6:00 PM. Here are some additional tips on planning practice sessions:

- **For students**: Practicing before doing homework provides a nice break between your academic activities, but it may be hard to focus on music if you have lots of homework to do.

- Waiting until after homework to practice may feel as if you're never finished; it's like **one obligation after the other**.

- Planning a practice session before your favorite TV show (which is then the **reward for practicing**) may be more successful than trying to get up and practice when the show is over.

### Holidays

It's really important that you keep to your practice sessions during (school) holidays as well. If you don't touch your instrument for a couple of weeks, the first lessons and practice sessions after the holiday may be quite frustrating as you probably won't be able to play those same pieces anymore. You may consider a holiday practice schedule, though.

### How?

People all have their own ways of handling assignments, most likely approaching them the same way they do other things in life. Teachers can help you apply your personal way of handling things to your practice sessions, making them as efficient as possible. Some examples:

* If you're not good at **focusing your attention**, don't start three new pieces at once.

* If you're afraid to **start new pieces**, you may tend to keep on 'practicing' songs you already play very well — so you're dedicating time to practicing, but you're not likely to make any progress.

* If you're not **aware of the mistakes** you make, you will end up rehearsing those mistakes, and it'll be hard to reverse and 'deprogram' those errors. The solution is to learn how to evaluate your own playing before moving on.

TIP

### Record your practice sessions

No matter how good you are, it's always hard to judge you own playing as you play. Tip: record your practice session, or your first or subsequent attempts to play the piece that you have been practicing, and then judge your performance by listening to the recording, once or a couple of times. This is very instructive for musicians at any level.

## WHERE

168

Ideally, you should be able to practice whenever you feel like it, without being hindered and without hindering others. A practice space needn't be large, just enough to accommodate you and your instrument. If there's room for the instrument to remain unpacked between practice sessions, no valuable time (or inspiration!) gets lost by having to unpack and assemble it before each practice. Ideally, again, you should be able to grab your instrument, tune it if necessary, and play. There are various types of floor-standing and wall-mounted stands on which string, wind, and other small instruments can sit unpacked and out of the way of people, pets and other damaging circumstances. Special covers are also available to help protect your valuable investments against dust and air-borne dirt.

### Music stand

If you read sheet music, you will need a music stand. This affordable piece of hardware promotes good posture (and prevents sore necks), provided it has been set up at the correct height. Nearly all music stands can be folded into a compact size, but it's easier if they can be left standing for the next practice session. This also enhances their life expectancy, as they may be quite flimsy. Do you need to bring a stand to lessons or recitals? Then invest in a second stand to be kept in the instrument case or bag, if possible, so you can't forget to bring it.

### More on music stands

A basic music stand will set you back less than twenty dollars. *Tip:* Most music stands have two 'arms' that keep the sheet music in place and prevent music books from flopping closed. If yours doesn't, you can use a rubber band or clothes pins, or you can have your music books spiral-bound so that they stay open. One more tip: Music stands are also available in bright colors and heavy-duty versions.

### Light

Lighting in the room should be sufficient to see the music easily and clearly. An additional small lamp is usually all that takes. Tip: There are special lamps available for music stands specifically.

### Stool or chair

A regular stool or chair will usually do. Pianists, keyboard players, drummers, and other musicians are better off using a special (preferably height-adjustable) stool or bench. Without it, posture may be bad and practicing can be tiresome.

**169**

TIP

### Metronome

*A metronome (see page 26) can help you develop your inner clock. It's also a great device to use when practicing entire pieces or difficult bits very slowly, and it can help you improve your speed on the instrument step by step. Like any other tool, metronomes should be used wisely. Using one isn't a very good idea with a new piece, or when you're focusing on your tone, for example. Also, if you use it too often, you may become dependent on it. Metronomes are available starting at less than twenty dollars.*

*Many electronic versions also sound a 440 Hz tuning tone (the standard A to which most instruments are tuned; see page 104).*

### Electronic tuner

Guitarists and many bassists usually rely on electronic tuners to help them tune their instrument. The more advanced types of *chromatic tuners* have a display that indicates which note (string) is being played, and whether it is flat (too low; the string needs to be tightened a bit) or sharp (too high; the string should be loosened a bit).

### For bowed instruments

These tuners can also be used for bowed string instruments, using the tuner's built in microphone rather than the instrument input. A basic tuner will typically set you back some twenty dollars. More expensive models with additional features are available as well. Some tuners double as a metronome.

### Vibrational tuners

Do you have to tune your cello onstage? Vibrational tuners only pick up the pitch from the instrument they're attached to. You simply clip this type of tuner to the headstock or the body of your instrument: Instead of a microphone, it has one or more sensors that pick up the instrument's vibrations.

### Tuning fork

Orchestral string players and other musicians often prefer using a tuning fork. This is a short, two-pronged fork that produces an A (or another specified pitch) when you tap it on your knee, and gently put the stem against your ear or on the bridge of your instrument.

### Sound systems and computers

Putting up a sound system in your practice area allows you to play along to prerecorded music, play back a recorded lesson, or maybe even record the practice session. Likewise, a computer can be used to play back CDs, DVDs, and CD-ROMS; to access Internet lessons and music games; or to record practice sessions (if equipped with the right hardware and software). It's also a helpful tool to compose, arrange, transpose, or create music. Synthesizers, home keyboards, and other digital instruments can be hooked up directly to the computer using MIDI, the musical instrument digital interface that is part of all digital music equipment.

### And more

There's much more you can do to make practice more effective and fun. Here are some additional tips:

- Consider **lightening up** on practice arrangements if you're very busy. Play your instrument to relax rather than to study.

- Try playing in **another room** of the house from time to time, or even outside, if possible.

- Make sure your practice time is **uninterrupted**, and ask people who call to call back.

- **Varying the structure** of your practice sessions can help keep things fresh. Have your main focus on playing a new piece for a month or so, then address sound production or intonation for a couple of weeks, and so on.

- If you want to practice an hour or more per day, do take one or **more short breaks**. Very brief micro-breaks help you stay focused. If you just can't get that one difficult passage down, comb your hair, pet the cat, eat a carrot, or take a sip of water before trying again. Or try again next week!

171

- Your instrument should be in good repair and tuned properly.

- Practicing with play-along recordings is often a lot more fun than practicing band or orchestra parts by yourself. There are commercially available play-along media, but another option is to record a performance or rehearsal of the band or orchestra you're in, and use that.

- Stop if it hurts. Playing an instrument should not induce pain. If the pain (back, fingers, neck, lips — anywhere) returns every time you practice or play, consult a teacher. The solution could be as simple as getting a different chair or resetting the music stand.

## THE COMPONENTS

One of the main keys to effective practice is to have well-structured practice sessions. Depending on your level of playing, the main components of a practice session are:

- Warming up
- Scales and arpeggios
- Etudes
- Sight-reading
- New pieces
- Review

If you're a beginning student, the list will be shorter, and elements will be added as you progress.

### Tuning

Most instruments need to be tuned, or the tuning needs to be checked, before you can play. This is where the practice session really begins. As said before, it is easiest if the instrument is always ready to be played — unpacked and assembled. You may want to have valuable and vulnerable instruments covered or packed when they're not being played, however. Also, parts such as strings, and the leather pads on woodwind instruments, tend to last longer if the instrument is covered between practice sessions.

### Warming up

Playing music requires a warm up, just like sports do: You may even get injured if you play demanding pieces without a decent warm up. For beginners and intermediate players, the few minutes of 'warming up' are basically meant to get into mood for playing, to get the fingers going, and to get 'into the instrument.' In that sense, it even helps if you take a good long look at your instrument before you play your first notes. Warm-up exercises are not technically demanding; they're the ideal setting for focusing on tone quality, because you can really listen to the sound you're producing.

### Scales, arpeggios and etudes

Scales and *arpeggios* (broken chords) are often used for warm ups, but they're also practiced separately. They're technical exercises that increase your playing proficiency, so your fingers will be able to do what your mind tells them to. Etudes are pieces written with that same goal in mind.

### More fun

Many musicians dislike playing scales, etudes, and similar exercise material; it's not as much fun as 'real' pieces, and such exercises often seem meaningless. A good teacher may be able to make you understand why they're so essential, inspiring you to play them with all your heart (though a little less will usually do). Besides, there are various ways to make playing scales and etudes more fun. Some ideas?

- **Focusing on your tone** really helps; imagine what a scale would sound like when played by your all-time favorite musician!

- Playing scales as if they were **beautiful pieces of music** makes a difference too.

- Make the **volume go up** as you play the scale upwards, and vice versa.

173

- **Speed up** when playing upwards, and vice versa.

- Speed up and **get louder** one way, and vice versa.

- Play scales in the rhythm of **a song you like**, or play them as triplets.

- Pianists: Play F-major with **your left hand** and C-major with **your right hand**, and experiment with other pairs of scales.

**TIP**

### New pieces

*Adding new pieces is necessary to keep progressing, to keep yourself challenged, to expand your repertoire, and to raise your general level of playing. Check pages 178–180 for tips on handling new pieces.*

### Reviewing repertoire

When you play pieces you already know, there's no struggle, so you're simply playing music. It's as close to performing as practicing will get — and that's what playing is all about, for most musicians. Reviewing older pieces also keeps your repertoire alive.

### Sight-reading

Sight-reading is as essential part of various exams and competitions: You're given a new and unfamiliar piece of music to read and play or sing on demand. It's much the same as reading a story or an article to someone, albeit that playing while reading music is quite a bit harder than reading text aloud. Sight-reading is an important skill for all musicians who want or need to play in situations where they will be expected to perform or rehearse without prior preparation.

### And more

A practicing session can consist of lots of other components, such as:

- **Specific exercises** (dynamics, phrasing, improvisation, ear training, extending your range with higher or lower notes, etc.).

**174**

- **Experimenting**: Explore the instrument, try to discover new sounds or playing techniques, try to figure out a melody you've heard, think up new melodies...

- **Playing along** with prerecorded music. Numerous self-taught players learned their instrument this way, and it's a valid, fun, and effective technique for any musician who doesn't have a band or an orchestra at their disposal.

### Recitals

Have you added a new piece to your repertoire and can you really play it? Again, try playing for friends or housemates. These brief, informal recitals can be very effective. They offer you an opportunity to perform, they may help diminish performance anxiety and they teach you to continue playing through mistakes — and you're most likely to make at least a few of those the first time you play a new piece.

### Maintenance

Some instruments require a bit of maintenance at the end of each practice session. Wind instruments have to be disassembled and dried, orchestral string instruments will need the hair of their bows slackened, guitar and bass guitar strings need to be cleaned, and so on. Specific instructions can be found in the relevant chapter of this Tipbook.

# STRUCTURE

To get the most out of your practice sessions, you need to structure them, planning ahead what it is you want to get done.

### The beginning and the end

It's usually best to start with things that are relatively easy to play, such as scales. You may also prefer to start each session with a piece you already know. Starting off with an unfamiliar piece can be quite frustrating. Ending the session with a review of familiar repertoire is like a reward for having practiced.

**175**

### The same order?
You may prefer the safety of doing things in the same order every time; others dislike such routine and rather vary the order of their practice components from day to day.

**TIP**

> ## Two or three sessions
>
> *If you divide your practice time into two or more sessions, it's often most effective to do a little of everything in each session rather then spending the first session on scales, the second on nothing but a new piece, etc.*

### Clock?
Some experts advise you to dedicate a certain amount of time to each component: a five minute warm-up, ten minutes on etudes, ten on a new piece, and another five to play something familiar. Others will tell you to get rid of the clock, as you want to focus on what you're playing rather than on the minutes passing by.

### Short, medium, long
The clearer your musical goals are, the easier it will be to practice effectively. When defining these goals, it often helps to distinguish:

- **Long-term goals**: I'd like to join such-and-such band, or play a solo recital by the end of the year or this month…

- **Mid-term goals**: I'd like to finish this method book, or be able to play these pieces…

- And **short-term goals**, which may differ for each practice session: I'd like to memorize this piece, or play that section ten times without a mistake…

# PRACTICING TECHNIQUES

Practicing efficiently is also a matter of applying the right practicing techniques. Improving your tone requires a different technique than increasing your speed, or tackling a new piece.

### Small jobs

One of the best ways to make your practice session more effective and fun is to break down large jobs into a number of small jobs. Rather than tackling a new piece from beginning to end, break it down into four or eight measures to be played per day, for example. This way, you can have a small success every day, rather than fighting to master the entire piece in one week.

### Revision

If a new piece is broken up into sections comprised of a number of bars, reviewing the sections that were done on previous days should be an essential part of each practice session. Learning an instrument is most effectively done through frequent repetition. (In various languages, the word for 'practice' literally means repetition!)

### The right notes

Repetition results in long-term memory storage, which is good. The problem, however, is that your memory does not select what should be stored and what should not. If you consistently repeat an incorrect passage, that's what will be stored, and if you play the wrong note half of the time, there's a fifty-fifty chance that the wrong note will come out at your performance. So when repeating things, make sure you play the right notes — and slow down as much as you need in order to do so.

### Five or ten

Some teachers may advise you to move to the next section only when you're able to play the current section correctly five (or ten) times in a row. If you make a mistake, you start counting all over again — until you get all five (or ten) correct. Others may not be concerned with the number of repetitions, so long as you play it right the final time: This way, your fingers are supposed to 'remember' the right moves.

### Slow down

A difficult passage may be hard to play correctly, and playing it right five times in a row may seem impossible. The solution, again, is to slow things down. Slow, in this case, means really slow. Take

177

one, two, or more seconds for every note, and disregard note values for now. Take a metronome, set it at sixty BPM (i.e., sixty Beats Per Minute, equaling one beat per second), and let it tick one, two, or more times before moving on to the next note. Such slow tempos make you aware of the movements your fingers have to make to get from note to note, or from chord to chord.

### Tone

For advanced players, practicing a piece really slowly is also a good way to work on their tone, and to get the smallest nuances of a piece right: dynamics, intonation, phrasing, and everything else beyond hitting the right notes at the right time.

# A NEW PIECE

There are also various practicing techniques for handling new pieces. As mentioned before, a piece can be divided up into four bar, eight bar, or longer sections, revising the previous sections (and playing them absolutely correctly) before moving on. This is just one of many approaches, and all of these approaches can be mixed to come up with a combination that is most effective for you.

### Challenge

Starting a new piece is a positive challenge to some, while it makes others feel as if they have to start all over again. Of course, avoiding new pieces will yield no progress. Also, learning to tackle new pieces can help you tackle other problems and deal with new, complex subjects as well — which is just one of the reasons that music students perform better in various academic fields. Some of the tips below apply to more advanced musicians only; others work for beginners too.

### Listen

As said before, it is essential that you practice a piece playing only the correct notes. It helps if you can first listen to a recorded version of the new piece so you know what it's supposed to sound like before attempting to play it. Of course, you can also ask your teacher to play the piece for you.

TIP

### Read along

*Reading along while listening to a new piece helps you link the notes to the music. With complex pieces, study the part visually before listening to it, so you won't be surprised by repeats and other markings. Reading the music before playing it also gives you the opportunity to check out all dynamic signs and tempo markings, to locate accidentals (flats, sharps, naturals), and numerous other details and characteristics of the piece — and you don't have to worry about playing the instrument at the same time you're reading.*

### More

If you have a teacher, ask him or her to tell you about the new piece of music: its general character, its form (12-bar blues or 32-bar AABA? Rondo or suite?), the style, the composer, the era in which it was written, and so on. After all, there's more to music than simply executing the composer's notes.

### Step by step

Beginning players are often advised to approach a new piece step by step. First, clap the rhythm of the notes, counting aloud as you go. When you've got the rhythm down, play the melody without paying attention to the rhythm. Once you can clap the rhythm and play the right notes, combine the two — very, very slowly. This approach works well for advanced players too. Pianists and other keyboard players can practice the left hand part first, and then the right hand, before attempting to play a new piece with both hands.

### The trouble spots

Alternatively, depending on your ability and the complexity of the piece, you can play the piece through at an easy tempo, spotting

**179**

the difficult bits as you go. Playing a piece as such, with mistakes and all, may give you a general idea of what it is about (assuming you haven't heard it before). Other players rather start by locating the tricky bits and figure them out first. A tip: If you're working on a tricky section, always include a few notes or bars before and after that particular section in order to make the tricky section a part of the whole thing, rather than an isolated hurdle that might scare you off every time you see it coming.

### Analyzing the trouble spots

If you're having a problem with a certain section, you can simply play it again and again (and again) until you get it right. However, it might be more effective to find out what's causing the problem in the first place. Is it the fingering (which fingers to use for which note)? The rhythm? Or can you not play the part with your left hand while your right hand is doing something else? Or is it a note higher or lower than you can play or sing? Without proper answers to those questions, it will be hard to move on — and before you get to the answers, you need to come up with the right questions. Again, this is something a teacher may be able to help you with. One step beyond analyzing the trouble spots is developing exercises that help the student tackle them. This is something advanced players do for themselves, and something that teachers should teach their students.

# MEMORIZING MUSIC

Opinions differ as to whether you should memorize music. Some teachers insist that you should; others feel that memorizing music should be optional, unless you're considering a professional career in music.

### Why?

Why would you learn to memorize a piece that you can simply read?

- It can help make you **a better musician**. If you don't have to focus on reading, you can fully focus on other elements

— tone, phrasing, dynamics, and so on — and listen to yourself play. Also, to play from memory you have to really know a piece inside out, which can only help improve your performance.

- Guitarists, pianists (and other keyboard players), and harpists who play by heart can **watch their hands** as they play, which may be very helpful if they have to make big leaps. Not a very professional approach, but it can be handy.

- It makes you **look good**. Professional soloists play without sheet music, so why can't you?

### Why not?
Of course, there's no need to keep musicians from memorizing music (and some are extremely good at it), but why force them?

- Being required to play without sheet music makes a performance an **even more stressful** event — and wasn't making music about enjoying yourself?

- Worrying about what'll happen if you forget the piece does not inspire a good performance. It **takes away more energy** from the music than reading notes does. In other words, some just need sheet music to play well, even while others might play better without it.

- If you're not good at memorizing music, learning pieces by heart may **take up valuable time** that's probably better spent on things you can do to grow musically. Do note that learning to memorize music takes time too: It's not something you just can do.

### Techniques and tips
There are various ways and techniques to memorize music. What works great for you, may not work for your friend, and vice versa. The following shortlist helps you recognize how typically handle things, and offers some suggestions.

- You can memorize a piece **as you learn it**, or you can wait to memorize it once you can play it correctly.

- Memorize **small sections at a time**. For some, a small section is

**181**

one or two bars; for others, it's half a page. Start with the first section, and add subsequent sections only after you've mastered previous sections.

- Some memorize **the difficult parts first**, repeating them so often that they become as easy to play as the rest of the piece. Only after mastering the difficult parts do they include the other sections. Tip: Many teachers claim that you should never play a piece in any other order than the one intended.

- Most musicians memorize a piece from **beginning to the end**, but there are those who prefer to do it the other way around, working their way back to the beginning.

- You can also **memorize bits and pieces as you go**. Try not to look at the music while you're playing, glancing up only as you feel you need to. Bit by bit, over time, you will learn to play the entire piece by heart.

- If you repeat a piece or a section over and over, you're using your **finger memory or tactile memory**. Your fingers know what to do because they've been trained to execute the patterns that are required for that piece of music. It's a relatively easy way to memorize, but it's not very reliable. Changing the tempo of the piece may confuse you (or your fingers). If you want to know if you've really memorized the music, play it at an extremely slow tempo and see what happens.

- Alternatively, you can analyze the piece **step by step**, studying every single aspect of it. This requires a lot of knowledge (scales, harmony, etc.), but it's the most reliable way to memorize.

- Practicing a piece **away from your instrument** may help you memorize it. Just play it in your imagination, first with, then without the music. This is referred to as shadow practicing or armchair memorizing. You can also try to hear the piece in your head without playing it, before you go to sleep, or on your way to work. Or sing it while you're taking a shower.

- It also helps if you **make up a story** that fits the music!

- **Slow practicing** is good for memorizing music.

182

- And when you're almost done, **put the book away**. Don't leave it on the music stand, pretending or trying not to peek, but put it in the other room. Out of sight, out of mind? Then try again.

*This chapter was taken from* Tipbook Music for Kids and Teens *(see page 207) and adapted for* Tipbook Cello.

# Glossary

This glossary briefly explains all the jargon touched on
so far. It also contains some terms that haven't been
mentioned yet, but which you may come across in other
books, in magazines, or on the Internet. Most terms are
explained in more detail as they are introduced in this
book. Please consult the index on pages 201–202.

**Adjuster**
See: *Fine tuners* and *Screw button*.

**Antiquing**
Technique to make cellos look older than they are.

**Back, back plate**
See: *Flamed wood* and *Top*.

**Baroque cello**
Special, mellow-sounding gut-stringed cello to play the music of the Baroque era.

**Bass bar**
Wooden bar on the inside of the top.

**Belly**
See: *Top*.

**Body**
The body consists of the top, the back, and the sides.

**Bottom nut**
See: *Saddle*.

**Bow**
Cellos are played with a bow. The bow is very important for the sound of the instrument. See also: *Bow hair*, *Frog*, and *Stick*.

**Bow grip**
Piece of (synthetic) leather wrapped around the stick of the bow. The term bow grip often refers to the (silver, silk, or imitation baleen) winding or lapping next to it as well. Also known as *thumb grip*.

**Bow hair**
The hair of the bow; either horsehair or synthetic. Also known as ribbon.

**Bridge**
The strings run over the bridge, which passes their vibrations on to the top.

**Button**
See: *Heel*.

**C-bout**
The waist of the body.

**Catgut**
The oldest material used for cello strings — sheep gut. The name comes from cattle gut.

**Cello in the white**
Unfinished cello.

**Channel**
The 'valley' near the edge of both the top and the back before the upward arching begins.

**Cheeks**
The sides of the pegbox.

**Children's cellos**
See: *Fractional sizes*.

**Curl**
See: *Flamed wood*.

**Double bass**
The lowest-sounding string instrument.

**Ebony**
See: *Wood*.

186

**Electric cello**
An electric cello can be plugged straight into an amplifier, just like an electric guitar.

**End pin**
The cello rests on a retractable, adjustable rod mounted in a (usually) wooden plug (end button). Plug and rod are collectively referred to as the end pin. Also known as spike.

**End screw**
See: *Screw button.*

**Eye, Parisian eye**
Inlaid decoration on tuning pegs, frogs, and other parts.
A Parisian eye is a mother-of-pearl dot with a small metal ring around it.

**ƒ-hole**
The soundholes of a cello are shaped like an *f*.

**F-stop**
See: *String length.*

**Figured wood**
See: *Flamed wood.*

**Fine tuners**
Small, additional tuning mechanisms in the tailpiece. Also referred to as tuning adjusters, string tuners, and string adjusters.

**Fingerboard**
When you play, you press down or stop the strings against the fingerboard.

**Fittings**
Collective name for the cello's replaceable parts, e.g., tailpiece, pegs, and nut, but the fingerboard as well. Also known as the trim.

**Flamed wood**
Many cellos have a back and ribs which look as though they have been 'licked by flames.' This flamed, figured, or curled wood is usually more expensive than plain wood.

**Fractional sizes**
Cellos in small or proportional sizes, designed for children. Fractional-sized instruments require fractional-sized strings

**Frog**
One end of the bow hair is held in place inside the frog. The underslide lines up with the top of the frog. At the bottom of the frog is the slide. Most frogs are full-lined with a metal back plate. At the front, where the hair enters the frog, it passes through the ferrule or D-ring.

**Full-size cello**
The regular, 4/4-size cello. See also: *Fractional sizes.*

**Fully-carved**
Fully-carved instruments have tops and backs made by carving only.

**Hair**
See: *Bow hair.*

**Heel**
Semi-circular projection of the back,

187

strengthening the joint of the body and the neck. Also referred to as the button.

**Lining**
Thin strips of wood glued to the inside edges of the body.

**Luthier**
Another name for a (master) violin maker.

**Maple**
See: *Wood*.

**Master cello**
Built by a master violin maker from start to finish.

**Mensur ratio**
See: *String length*.

**Mountings**
The metal parts of a bow.

**Mute**
A mute makes your sound a little sweeter and softer. Practice mutes muffle the sound a lot.

**Neck**
The long wooden section that extends from the body. The fingerboard is attached to the neck.

**Nickel silver**
Mixture of copper, zinc, and nickel. Also known as alpaca.

**Nut**
The wooden strip over which the strings run at the top end of the neck. Also called top nut.

**Parisian eye**
See: *Eye, Parisian eye*.

**Peg, Pegbox**
The (tuning) pegs are fitted into the pegbox. See also: *Tuning pegs*.

**Peg compound**
Lubricant for tuning pegs.

**Peg dope**
Lubricant for tuning pegs.

**Pegging**
The process of fitting the tuning pegs to the instrument.

**Pickup**
Small, thin sensor that converts the vibrations of your strings into electrical signals, so that you can plug your cello into an amplifier.

**Plain wood**
See: *Flamed wood*.

**Plates**
The back and the top or table of the instrument.

**Practice mute**
See: *Mute*.

**Proportional instruments**
See: *Fractional sizes*.

**Purfling**
Inlaid decoration; also protects the top and back.

**Quartered wood, quarter-sawn wood**
If you saw a tree trunk or sections

of it into quarters (the way you would cut a cake into slices), you get stronger wood than if you slab-cut the tree.

Because wood or quartered wood is stronger, it is good for making thin yet strong and stable tops and backs.

**Ribbon**
See: *Bow hair.*

**Ribs**
The sides of the body.

**Romberg**
Romberg fingerboards have a flat area under the C-string.

**Rosin**
Without rosin to make the bow hair sticky, your bow will do nothing at all.

**Saddle**
A strip, usually of ebony, that prevents the top from being damaged by the loop that holds the tailpiece in place. Also known as bottom nut.

**Screw button**
Used to tighten and relax the bow hair. Also called end screw or adjuster.

**Scroll**
The head of the instrument. Often referred to as the maker's signature.

**Slide**
See: *Frog.*

**Sound post**
Thin, cylindrical piece of wood wedged between top and back of the instrument. Referred to as the 'soul' of the cello.

**Spike**
See: *End pin.*

**Spruce**
See: *Wood.*

**Stick**
The main wooden — or synthetic — part of your bow.

**Stop**
See: *String length.*

**Stradivarius**
Antonio Stradivari, often referred to as Stradivarius, is the world's most famous violin maker. He also built the standard model for the cello.

**String adjusters**
See: *Fine tuners.*

**String height**
The distance from the strings to the fingerboard, measured at the end nearest the bridge.

**String length**
Usually refers to the length of the strings between nut and bridge, also known as their speaking length. Violin makers also use the term f-stop, referring to the distance from the top edge of the body to the notches of the *f*-holes. The ratio between the distance from

189

the body's edge to the notches and from the nut to the edge is referred to as the stop, neck to stop ratio, or mensur ratio.

In cellos the mensur ratio is usually 10:7, but differences may occur, even between cellos with identical string lengths. A tip: A deviant mensur ratio can make you play out of tune at first.

**String tuners**
See: *Fine tuners.*

**Strings**
Cello strings are available in gut, synthetic-core, and steel-core versions, and with windings made of all kinds of metals.

**Table**
See: *Top.*

**Tailgut**
See: *Tailpiece, tailpiece loop.*

**Tailpiece, tailpiece loop**
The strings are attached to the tailpiece, and the tailpiece is attached to the end button with the tailpiece loop or tailgut.

**Top**
One of the most important components of a cello: the top of the body, also known as table or belly. The opposite side is the back.

**Top nut**
See: *Nut.*

**Trim**
See: *Fittings.*

**Tuning**
Cellos are tuned using the tuning pegs or the fine tuners.

**Tuning adjusters**
See: *Fine tuners.*

**Tuning pegs**
Cellos have a tuning peg (often simply called peg) for each string, sometimes in combination with a fine tuner. The peg head is known as the *thumb piece*. See also: *Fine tuners.*

**Underslide**
See: *Frog.*

**Varnish**
The varnish used on a cello is important for its sound and appearance. Certain varnishes may require certain cleaning methods over others. Check with a violin maker or professional.

**Viola, violin**
Two very close, much smaller relatives of the cello.

**Volute**
The spiral-shaped end of the scroll.

**White cello**
Unfinished cello.

**Winding**
See: *Bow grip* and *Wound strings.*

**Wolf tone**
A stuttering sound that affects many cellos. Wolf tones can be reduced in different ways.

**Wood**

The main types of wood used for cellos are spruce (for tops), maple (for backs and sides) and ebony (for fingerboards, tuning pegs, tailpieces, and other parts).

# TIPCODE LIST

The Tipcodes in this book offer easy access to short videos, sound files, and other additional information at www.tipbook.com. For your convenience, the Tipcodes in this Tipbook have been listed below.

| Tipcode | Topic | Chapter | Page |
|---------|-------|---------|------|
| CELLO-001 | A wide range | 1 | 2 |
| CELLO-002 | Many different styles | 1 | 3 |
| CELLO-003 | Stopping the strings | 2 | 8 |
| CELLO-004 | Pizzicato | 3 | 20 |
| CELLO-005 | Practice mute | 3 | 23 |
| CELLO-006 | Fine tuners | 5 | 55 |
| CELLO-007 | Spiccato | 7 | 83 |
| CELLO-008 | Flexibility | 7 | 84 |
| CELLO-009 | Tuning fork | 9 | 105 |
| CELLO-010 | Harmonic (octave) | 9 | 106 |
| CELLO-011 | String pitches | 9 | 107 |
| CELLO-012 | Adjacent strings | 9 | 108 |
| CELLO-013 | Adjacent harmonics | 9 | 108 |
| CELLO-014 | Tuning with pegs | 9 | 111 |
| CELLO-015 | A-concert pitch (440Hz) | 9 | 112 |
| CELLO-016 | 440 and 442 Hz: the difference | 9 | 112 |
| CELLO-017 | Applying rosin | 10 | 117 |
| CELLO-018 | Removing strings | 10 | 121 |
| CELLO-019 | Fitting strings | 10 | 123 |
| CELLO-020 | Violin | 12 | 142 |
| CELLO-021 | Double bass | 12 | 142 |

# Want to Know More?

Tipbooks supply you with basic information on the instrument of your choice, and everything that comes with it. Of course there's a lot more to be found on all of the subjects you came across on these pages. This section offers a selection of magazines, books, helpful websites, and more.

## MAGAZINES

The following magazines offer lots of articles on cellos, violin makers, strings, playing, and much more.

• *Strings*, www.stringsmagazine.com.

• *The Journal of the Violin Society of America*, www.vsa.to (also see below).

• *The Strad* (UK), www.thestrad.com.

• *American Lutherie*, www.luth.org (stringed instrument making and repair; covers guitars and other fretted instruments as well).

• *Stringendo*, Australian Strings Association, www.austa.asn.au.

## BOOKS

There are dozens of books on the cello. In some cases, the title lists the violin only — but cellos are covered as well.
The following list is a brief selection of publications that cover some of the subjects of this Tipbook in greater depth.

• *Cello* (Yehudi Menuhin Music Guides), by William Pleeth (Kahn & Averill, 2001; 290 pages; ISBN 1 871 08238 2).

• *Cambridge Companion to the Cello*, Robin Stowell (editor) (Cambridge University Press, 2000; 269 pages; ISBN 0 521 62928 4).

• *Cello Story*, by Dimitri Markevitch (Summy Brichards Inc., 1984; 182 pages; ISBN 0 874 87406 8).

• *The Cello*, by Elizabeth Cowling (B.T. Batsford, 1975; 224 pages; ISBN 0 713 42879 1).

• *The Health of the Violin, Viola & Cello: Practical Advice on the Acquisition, Maintenance, Adjustment, & Conservation of Bowed Instruments*, by Lucien Greilsamer (Henry Strobel, Violin Maker and Publisher, 1991; ISBN 0 962 06734 2).

• *The Violin Explained – Components, Mechanism and Sound*, by Sir James Beament (Oxford University Press, 2000; 264 pages; ISBN 0 198 16623 0).

194

### Making a cello

There are quite a few books for amateur and professional violin makers, which also can be of interest if you just want to know more about the instrument — be it a violin or a cello. Some examples:

- *Cello Making, Step by Step*, by Henry Strobel (1995; ISBN 0 962 06737 7). This book should be used with *Violin Making, Step by Step* (1994; ISBN 0 962 06736 9). The author and publisher of these titles, Henry Strobel, wrote various other books on the subject as well.

- *Violin Making: A Guide for the Amateur*, by Bruce Ossman (Fox Chapel Publications, 1998; 96 pages; ISBN 1 565 23091 4).

- *Violin and Cello Building & Repairing*, by Robert Alton (Library Binding; 182 pages; ISBN 0781205174).

- *Violin Making, a Practical Guide*, by Juliet Barker (The Crowood Press, 2001; 128 pages; ISBN 1 861 26436 4).

### INTERNET

On the Internet, you'll find countless sites for cellists, often with all kinds of links, articles, discussion groups, and FAQs. Following are some good starting points:

- Internet Cello Society (www.cello.org)

- New Directions Cello Association (www.newdirectionscello.com)

- American String Teachers Association (www.astaweb.com)

- Maestronet (www.maestronet.com)

- American Federation of Violin and Bow Makers (www.afvbm.com)

- Cello Heaven (www.celloheaven.com)

- The Joy of Cello Playing (www.wimmercello.com)

- Jazz String Caucus (www.JazzStringCaucus.org)

**195**

### Smithsonian Institution

Of course, you can also check out whether there is anything on the maker of your cello by searching the Internet on that name. If you are interested in the great old masters, take a look at The Smithsonian Institution's site at www.si.edu and search for 'cellos' or 'violins.'

### Looking for a teacher?

The Internet can also help you find a teacher. You may try to search for "cello teacher" and the name of area or city where you live, consult your national string teachers association (see below), or visit one of the following special interest websites:

- PrivateLessons.com: www.privatelessons.com

- MusicStaff.com: www.musicstaff.com

- The Music Teachers List: www.teachlist.com

- Private Music Instructor National Directory: www.oberwerk.com/pmind

### ASSOCIATIONS

- The Violin Society Of America (VSA; 1974) promotes the art and science of making, repairing, and preserving the instruments and bows of the violin family. The VSA organizes an annual convention that features speakers, demonstrations of instrument and bow making and repair, performances, and more. For information please visit www.vsa.to. The VSA also publishes a journal (see above) and a quarterly newsletter.

- The Australian Strings Association (www.austa.asn.au.home. html) is a similar organization for professional and amateur instrumentalists, schools and institutions, teachers, students, conductors, and repairers and makers of string instruments.

- There are various associations of string teachers, such as the American String Teachers Association (www.astaweb.com) and the European String Teachers Association (www.esta-int. com). The British Branch of the European String Teachers Association can be found at www.estaweb.org.uk.

### Violin makers

If you want to locate a professional violin maker, contact
the American Federation of Violin and Bow Makers
(www.afvbm.com); check out the Directory of Australian Violin
and Bow Makers at www.abcviolins.com; or contact the British
Violin Making Association (www.bvma.org.uk), for example.
Similar organizations and directories can be found in other
countries too.

# ESSENTIAL DATA

*In the event of your instrument being stolen or lost, or if you just decide to sell it, it's useful to have all the relevant data at hand, either for yourself, your insurance company, or for the police. You can jot down this information on these three pages. There's also room to list the strings you're currently using, for future reference.*

## INSURANCE

Insurance company:

Phone:                                        Email:

Broker:

Phone:                                        Email:

Policy no.:

Premium:

## CELLO

You'll find some of the details of your cello on the label, which — if there is one — is usually visible through the *f*-hole on the side of the C-string. Some cellos have labels that can only be read when the body is opened. The name of the maker can also be branded in the body, for example on the back, close to the heel.

Make and model:

Manufacturer/violin maker:

Serial number:

Color:

Make of bridge:

## TAILPIECE

Make:

Type:

Color/material:

## DESCRIPTION OF TUNING PEGS:

## ACCESSORIES AND OTHER INSTRUMENTS

| | |
|---|---|
| Date of purchase: | Price: |
| Place of purchase: | |
| Phone: | Email: |

## BOW

| | |
|---|---|
| Make/maker: | |
| Type: | Price: |
| Octagonal/round: | |
| Mounting: | |
| Date of purchase: | |
| Place of purchase: | |
| Phone: | |

## STRINGS

It's worth making a note of the strings you put on your cello, so you can use the same ones again if you like them — or avoid them if you don't.

| STRING | MAKE | TYPE | THICKNESS/TENSION | DATE |
|---|---|---|---|---|
| 1st: A | | | | |
| 2nd: D | | | | |
| 3rd: G | | | | |
| 4th: C | | | | |

| STRING | MAKE | TYPE | THICKNESS/TENSION | DATE |
|---|---|---|---|---|
| 1st: A | | | | |
| 2nd: D | | | | |
| 3rd: G | | | | |
| 4th: C | | | | |

| STRING | MAKE | TYPE | THICKNESS/TENSION | DATE |
|---|---|---|---|---|
| 1st: A | | | | |
| 2nd: D | | | | |
| 3rd: G | | | | |
| 4th: C | | | | |

| STRING | MAKE | TYPE | THICKNESS/TENSION | DATE |
|---|---|---|---|---|
| 1st: A | | | | |
| 2nd: D | | | | |
| 3rd: G | | | | |
| 4th: C | | | | |

**ADDITIONAL NOTES**

# INDEX

*Please check out the glossary on pages 185-191 for additional definitions of the terms used in this book.*

**201**

# THE TIPBOOK SERIES

*Did you like this Tipbook? There are also Tipbooks for your fellow band or orchestra members! The Tipbook Series features various books on musical instruments, including the singing voice, in addition to Tipbook Music on Paper, Tipbook Amplifiers and Effects, and Tipbook Music for Kids and Teens – a Guide for Parents.*

*Every Tipbook is a highly accessible and easy-to-read compilation of the knowledge and expertise of numerous musicians, teachers, technicians, and other experts, written for musicians of all ages, at all levels, and in any style of music. Please check www.tipbook.com for up to date information on the Tipbook Series!*

*All Tipbooks come with Tipcodes that offer additional information, sound files and short movies at www.tipbook.com*

### Instrument Tipbooks

All instrument Tipbooks offer a wealth of highly accessible, yet well-founded information on one or more closely related instruments. The first chapters of each Tipbook explain the very basics of the instrument(s), explaining all the parts and what they do, describing what's involved in learning to play, and indicating typical instrument prices. The core chapters, addressing advanced players as well, turn you into an instant expert on the instrument. This knowledge allows you to make an informed purchase and get the most out of your instrument. Comprehensive chapters on maintenance, intonation, and tuning are also included, as well a brief section on the history, the family, and the production of the instrument.

### Tipbook Acoustic Guitar

*Tipbook Acoustic Guitar* explains all of the elements that allow you to recognize and judge a guitar's timbre, performance, and playability, focusing on both steel-string and nylon-string instruments. There are chapters covering the various types of strings and their characteristics, and there's plenty of helpful information on changing and cleaning strings, on tuning and maintenance, and even on the care of your fingernails.

**203**

### Tipbook Amplifiers and Effects – $14.95

Whether you need a guitar amp, a sound system, a multi-effects unit for a bass guitar, or a keyboard amplifier, *Tipbook Amplifiers and Effects* helps you to make a good choice. Two chapters explain general features (controls, equalizers, speakers, MIDI, etc.) and figures (watts, ohms, impedance, etc.), and further chapters cover the specifics of guitar amps, bass amps, keyboard amps, acoustic amps, and sound systems. Effects and effect units are dealt with in detail, and there are also chapters on microphones and pickups, and cables and wireless systems.

### Tipbook Cello – $14.95

Cellists can find everything they need to know about their instrument in *Tipbook Cello*. The book gives you tips on how to select an instrument and choose a bow, tells you all about the various types of strings and rosins, and gives you helpful tips on the maintenance and tuning of your instrument. Basic information on electric cellos is included as well!

### Tipbook Clarinet – $14.95

*Tipbook Clarinet* sheds light on every element of this fascinating instrument. The knowledge presented in this guide makes trying out and selecting a clarinet much easier, and it turns you into an instant expert on offset and in-line trill keys, rounded or French-style keys, and all other aspects of the instrument. Special chapters are devoted to reeds (selecting, testing, and adjusting reeds), mouthpieces and ligatures, and maintenance.

### Tipbook Electric Guitar and Bass Guitar – $14.95

Electric guitars and bass guitars come in many shapes and sizes. *Tipbook Electric Guitar and Bass Guitar* explains all of their features and characteristics, from neck profiles, frets, and types of wood to different types of pickups, tuning machines, and — of course — strings. Tuning and advanced do-it-yourself intonation techniques are included.

### Tipbook Drums – $14.95

A drum is a drum is a drum? Not true — and *Tipbook Drums* tells you all the ins and outs of their differences, from the type of wood to the dimensions of the shell, the shape of the bearing edge, and the drum's hardware. Special chapters discuss selecting drum sticks, drum heads, and cymbals. Tuning and muffling, two techniques a drummer must master to make the instrument sound as good as it can, are covered in detail, providing step-by-step instructions.

### Tipbook Flute and Piccolo – $14.95

Flute prices range from a few hundred to fifty thousand dollars and more. *Tipbook Flute and Piccolo* tells you how workmanship, materials, and other elements make for different instruments with vastly different prices, and teaches you how to find the instrument that best suits your or your child's needs. Open-hole or closed-hole keys, a B-foot or a C-foot, split-E or donut, inline or offset G? You'll be able to answer all these questions — and more — after reading this guide.

### Tipbook Keyboard and Digital Piano – $14.95

Buying a home keyboard or a digital piano may find you confronted with numerous unfamiliar terms. *Tipbook Keyboard and Digital Piano* explains all of them in a very easy-to-read fashion — from hammer action and non-weighted keys to MIDI, layers and splits, arpeggiators and sequencers, expression pedals and multi-switches, and more, including special chapters on how to judge the instrument's sound, accompaniment systems, and the various types of connections these instruments offer.

### Tipbook Music for Kids and Teens – a Guide for Parents – $14.95

How do you inspire children to play music? How do you inspire them to practice? What can you do to help them select an instrument, to reduce stage fright, or to practice effectively? What can you do to make practice fun? How do you reduce sound levels and

**205**

prevent hearing damage? These and many more questions are dealt with in *Tipbook Music for Kids and Teens – a Guide for Parents and Caregivers.* The book addresses all subjects related to the musical education of children from pre-birth to pre-adulthood.

### Tipbook Music on Paper – $14.95

*Tipbook Music on Paper – Basic Theory* offers everything you need to read and understand the language of music. The book presumes no prior understanding of theory and begins with the basics, explaining standard notation, but moves on to advanced topics such as odd time signatures and transposing music in a fashion that makes things really easy to understand.

### Tipbook Piano – $14.95

Choosing a piano becomes a lot easier with the knowledge provided in *Tipbook Piano*, which makes for a better understanding of this complex, expensive instrument without going into too much detail. How to judge and compare piano keyboards and pedals, the influence of the instrument's dimensions, different types of cabinets, how to judge an instrument's timbre, the difference between laminated and solid wood soundboards, accessories, hybrid and digital pianos, and why tuning and regulation are so important: Everything is covered in this handy guide.

### Tipbook Saxophone – $14.95

At first glance, all alto saxophones look alike. And all tenor saxophones do too — yet they all play and sound different from each other. *Tipbook Saxophone* discusses the instrument in detail, explaining the key system and the use of additional keys, the different types of pads, corks, and springs, mouthpieces and how they influence timbre and playability, reeds (and how to select and adjust them) and much more. Fingering charts are also included!

### Tipbook Trumpet and Trombone, Flugelhorn and Cornet – $14.95

The Tipbook on brass instruments focuses on the smaller horns listed in the title. It explains all of the jargon you come across when you're out to buy or rent an instrument, from bell material to the shape of the bore, the leadpipe, valves and valve slides, and all other elements of the horn. Mouthpieces, a crucial choice for the sound and playability of all brasswinds, are covered in a separate chapter.

### Tipbook Violin and Viola – $14.95

*Tipbook Violin and Viola* covers a wide range of subjects, ranging from an explanation of different types of tuning pegs, fine tuners, and tailpieces, to how body dimensions and the bridge may influence the instrument's timbre. Tips on trying out instruments and bows are included. Special chapters are devoted to the characteristics of different types of strings, bows, and rosins, allowing you to get the most out of your instrument.

### Tipbook Vocals – The Singing Voice – $14.95

*Tipbook Vocals –The Singing Voice* helps you realize the full potential of your singing voice. The book, written in close collaboration with classical and non-classical singers and teachers, allows you to discover the world's most personal and precious instrument without reminding you of anatomy class. Topics include breathing and breath support, singing loudly without hurting your voice, singing in tune, the timbre of your voice, articulation, registers and ranges, memorizing lyrics, and more. The main purpose of the chapter on voice care is to prevent problems.

### International editions

The Tipbook Series is also available in Spanish, French, German, Dutch, Italian, Swedish, and Chinese. For more information, please visit us at www.tipbook.com.

207

# TIPBOOK SERIES MUSIC AND MUSICAL INSTRUMENTS

**Tipbook Acoustic Guitar**
ISBN 978-1-4234-6523-2, HL00332802 — $14.95

**Tipbook Amplifiers and Effects**
ISBN 978-1-4234-6277-4, HL00332776 — $14.95

**Tipbook Cello**
ISBN 978-1-4234-5623-0, HL00331904 — $14.95

**Tipbook Clarinet**
ISBN 978-1-4234-6524-9, HL00332803 — $14.95

**Tipbook Drums**
ISBN 978-90-8767-102-0, HL00331474 — $14.95

**Tipbook Electric Guitar and Bass Guitar**
ISBN 978-1-4234-4274-5, HL00332372 — $14.95

**Tipbook Flute & Piccolo**
ISBN 978-1-4234-6525-6, HL00332804 — $14.95

**Tipbook Home Keyboard and Digital Piano**
ISBN 978-1-4234-4277-6, HL00332375 — $14.95

**Tipbook Music for Kids and Teens**
ISBN 978-1-4234-6526-3, HL00332805 — $14.95

**Tipbook Music on Paper  — Basic Theory**
ISBN 978-1-4234-6529-4, HL00332807 — $14.95

**Tipbook Piano**
ISBN 978-1-4234-6278-1, HL00332777 — $14.95

**Tipbook Saxophone**
ISBN 978-90-8767-101-3, HL00331475 — $14.95

**Tipbook Trumpet and Trombone, Flugelhorn and Cornet**
ISBN 978-1-4234-6527-0, HL00332806 — $14.95

**Tipbook Violin and Viola**
ISBN 978-1-4234-4276-9, HL00332374 — $14.95

**Tipbook Vocals — The Singing Voice**
ISBN 978-1-4234-5622-3, HL00331949 — $14.95

**Check www.tipbook.com for additional information!**